Kaplan Publishing are constantly finding r
looking for exam success and our online r
extra dimension to your studies.

This book comes with free MyKaplan onlir
study anytime, anywhere. **This free online resource is not sold
separately and is included in the price of the book.**

CW00401502

5

Having purchased this book, you have access to the following online study materials:

CONTENT	AAT	
	Text	Kit
Electronic version of the book	✓	✓
Knowledge Check tests with instant answers	✓	
Mock assessments online	✓	✓
Material updates	✓	✓

How to access your online resources

Kaplan Financial students will already have a MyKaplan account and these extra resources will be available to you online. You do not need to register again, as this process was completed when you enrolled. If you are having problems accessing online materials, please ask your course administrator.

If you are not studying with Kaplan and did not purchase your book via a Kaplan website, to unlock your extra online resources please go to www.mykaplan.co.uk/add-online-resources (even if you have set up an account and registered books previously). You will then need to enter the ISBN number (on the title page and back cover) and the unique pass key number contained in the scratch panel below to gain access. You will also be required to enter additional information during this process to set up or confirm your account details.

If you purchased through the Kaplan Publishing website you will automatically receive an e-mail invitation to MyKaplan. Please register your details using this email to gain access to your content. If you do not receive the e-mail or book content, please contact Kaplan Publishing.

Your Code and Information

This code can only be used once for the registration of one book online. This registration and your online content will expire when the final sittings for the examinations covered by this book have taken place. Please allow one hour from the time you submit your book details for us to process your request.

Please scratch the film to access your unique code.

Please be aware that this code is case-sensitive and you will need to include the dashes within the passcode, but not when entering the ISBN.

KAPLAN

PUBLISHING

AAT

Q2022

Management Accounting Techniques

EXAM KIT

This Exam Kit supports study for the following AAT qualifications:
AAT Level 3 Diploma in Accounting
AAT Level 3 Certificate in Bookkeeping
AAT Diploma in Accounting at SCQF Level 7

KAPLAN

PUBLISHING

British Library Cataloguing-in-Publication Data

A catalogue record for this book is available from the British Library.

Published by:

Kaplan Publishing UK

Unit 2 The Business Centre

Molly Millar's Lane

Wokingham

Berkshire

RG41 2QZ

ISBN: 978-1-83996-061-1

© Kaplan Financial Limited, 2021

Printed and bound in Great Britain

This Product includes content from the International Auditing and Assurance Standards Board (IAASB) and the International Ethics Standards Board for Accountants (IESBA), published by the International Federation of Accountants (IFAC) in 2015 and is used with permission of IFAC.

CONTENTS

Features in this revision kit

In addition to providing a wide ranging bank of real exam style questions, we have also included in this kit:

- unit specific information and advice on exam technique

- our recommended approach to make your revision for this particular subject as effective as possible.

You will find a wealth of other resources to help you with your studies on the AAT website:

www.aat.org.uk/

Quality and accuracy are of the utmost importance to us so if you spot an error in any of our products, please send an email to mykaplanreporting@kaplan.com with full details, or follow the link to the feedback form in MyKaplan.

Our Quality Co-ordinator will work with our technical team to verify the error and take action to ensure it is corrected in future editions.

UNIT SPECIFIC INFORMATION

THE EXAM

FORMAT OF THE ASSESSMENT

The assessment will comprise six independent tasks. Two of the tasks will be human marked. Students will normally be assessed by computer-based assessment.

In any one assessment, students may not be assessed on all content, or on the full depth or breadth of a piece of content. The content assessed may change over time to ensure validity of assessment, but all assessment criteria will be tested over time.

The learning outcomes for this unit are as follows:

	Learning outcome	Weighting
1	Understanding the purpose and use of management accounting within organisations	10%
2	Use techniques required for dealing with costs	15%
3	Attribute costs according to organisational requirements	20%
4	Investigate deviations from budget	15%
5	Use spreadsheet techniques to provide management accounting information	15%
6	Use management accounting techniques to support short-term decision making	15%
7	Understand principles of cash management	10%
	Total	100%

Time allowed

2 ½ hours

PASS MARK

The pass mark for all AAT CBAs is 70%.

 Always keep your eye on the clock and make sure you attempt all questions!

DETAILED SYLLABUS

The detailed syllabus and study guide written by the AAT can be found at:

www.aat.org.uk/

INDEX TO QUESTIONS AND ANSWERS

EXAM TECHNIQUE

- **Do not skip any of the material** in the syllabus.

- **Read each question** *very* carefully.

- **Double-check your answer** before committing yourself to it.

- Answer **every** question – if you do not know an answer to a multiple choice question or true/false question, you don't lose anything by guessing. Think carefully before you **guess**.

- If you are answering a multiple-choice question, **eliminate first those answers that you know are wrong**. Then choose the most appropriate answer from those that are left.

- **Don't panic** if you realise you've answered a question incorrectly. Getting one question wrong will not mean the difference between passing and failing.

Computer-based exams – tips

- Do not attempt a CBA until you have **completed all study material** relating to it.

- On the AAT website there is a CBA demonstration. It is **ESSENTIAL** that you attempt this before your real CBA. You will become familiar with how to move around the CBA screens and the way that questions are formatted, increasing your confidence and speed in the actual exam.

- Be sure you understand how to use the **software** before you start the exam. If in doubt, ask the assessment centre staff to explain it to you.

- Questions are **displayed on the screen** and answers are entered using keyboard and mouse. At the end of the exam, you are given a certificate showing the result you have achieved.

- In addition to the traditional multiple-choice question type, CBAs will also contain **other types of questions**, such as number entry questions, drag and drop, true/false, pick lists or drop down menus or hybrids of these.

- You need to be sure you **know how to answer questions** of this type before you sit the exam, through practice.

KAPLAN PUBLISHING

KAPLAN'S RECOMMENDED REVISION APPROACH

QUESTION PRACTICE IS THE KEY TO SUCCESS

Success in professional examinations relies upon you acquiring a firm grasp of the required knowledge at the tuition phase. In order to be able to do the questions, knowledge is essential.

However, the difference between success and failure often hinges on your exam technique on the day and making the most of the revision phase of your studies.

The **Kaplan textbook** is the starting point, designed to provide the underpinning knowledge to tackle all questions. However, in the revision phase, poring over text books is not the answer.

Kaplan pocket notes are designed to help you quickly revise a topic area; however you then need to practise questions. There is a need to progress to exam style questions as soon as possible, and to tie your exam technique and technical knowledge together.

The importance of question practice cannot be over-emphasised.

The recommended approach below is designed by expert tutors in the field, in conjunction with their knowledge of the examiner and the specimen assessment.

You need to practise as many questions as possible in the time you have left.

OUR AIM

Our aim is to get you to the stage where you can attempt exam questions confidently, to time, in a closed book environment, with no supplementary help (i.e. to simulate the real examination experience).

Practising your exam technique is also vitally important for you to assess your progress and identify areas of weakness that may need more attention in the final run up to the examination.

In order to achieve this we recognise that initially you may feel the need to practice some questions with open book help.

Good exam technique is vital.

THE KAPLAN REVISION PLAN

Stage 1: Assess areas of strengths and weaknesses

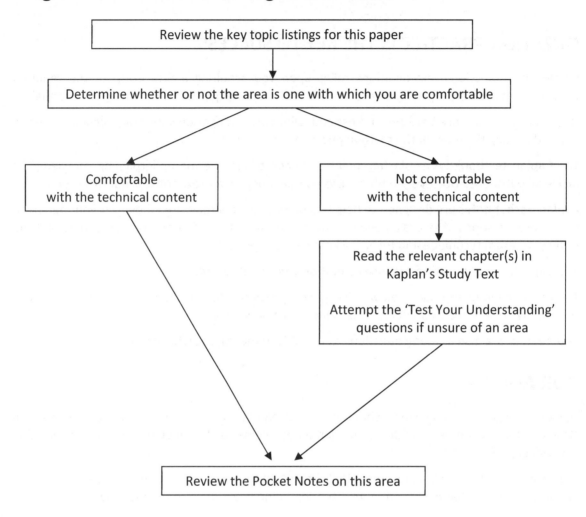

Stage 2: Practise questions

Follow the order of revision of topics as presented in this kit and attempt the questions in the order suggested.

Try to avoid referring to text books and notes and the model answer until you have completed your attempt.

Review your attempt with the model answer and assess how much of the answer you achieved.

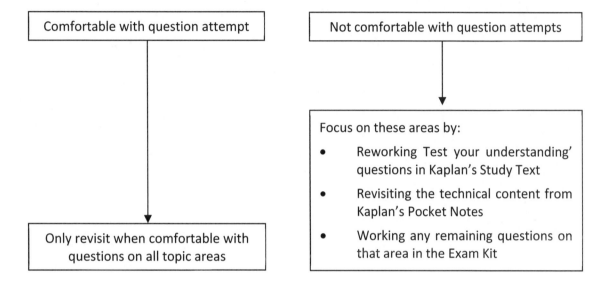

Stage 3: Final pre-exam revision

We recommend that you **attempt at least one two and a half hour mock examination** containing a set of previously unseen exam standard questions.

Attempt the mock CBA online in timed, closed book conditions to simulate the real exam experience.

Section 1

PRACTICE QUESTIONS

COSTING TECHNIQUES

MATERIALS

1 **Which of the following is least relevant to the simple economic order quantity model for inventory?**

    A   Safety inventory

    B   Annual demand

    C   Holding costs

    D   Ordering costs

2 The EOQ formula includes the cost of placing an order. However, the management accountant is unsure which of the following items would usually be included in 'cost of placing an order'

    (i)   administrative costs

    (ii)   postage

    (iii)   quality control costs

    (iv)   unit cost of products

    (v)   storekeeper's salary

Which three of the above would be regarded as part of the cost of placing an order?

    A   (i), (ii) and (iii)

    B   (i), (iv) and (v)

    C   (ii), (iii) and (iv)

    D   (i), (ii) and (v)

3   GLOBE LTD

Globe Ltd uses a standard component XZ7.

It estimates the following information regarding this component:

Weekly usage	1,500 – 3,500 units
Delivery period	2 – 4 weeks
Buffer (minimum) inventory	17,000 units
Maximum re-order quantity	15,750 units

Globe Ltd orders 11,250 components in each order.

Calculate the following:

(a)   Re-order level

(b)   Maximum inventory

(c)   Minimum re-order quantity

4   PLASTIC

The following information is available for plastic grade PM7:

- Annual demand 112,500 kilograms.

- Annual holding cost per kilogram £1.80

- Fixed ordering cost £3.60.

(a)   **Calculate the Economic Order Quantity (EOQ) for PM7 (round to the nearest whole number).**

The inventory record shown below for plastic grade PM7 for the month of July has only been fully completed for the first three weeks of the month.

(b)   **Complete the entries in the inventory record for the two receipts on 24 and 28 July that were ordered using the EOQ method.**

(c)   **Complete ALL entries in the inventory record for the two issues in the month and for the closing balance at the end of July using the FIFO method of issuing inventory.**

(Show the costs per kilogram (kg) in £'s to 3 decimal places; and the total costs in whole £'s).

Inventory record for plastic grade PM7

Date	Receipts			Issues			Balance	
	Quantity kgs	Cost per kg (£)	Total cost (£)	Quantity kgs	Cost per kg (£)	Total cost (£)	Quantity kgs	Total cost (£)
Balance as at 22 July							198	238
24 July		2.336						
26 July				540				
28 July		2.344						
30 July				710				

5 SURESTICK GLUE

The following information is available for direct material SURESTICK GLUE:

- Fixed ordering cost £2.50

- Annual holding cost per litre £1.00

- Monthly demand 2,500 litres.

(a) **Calculate the Economic Order Quantity (EOQ) for direct material SURESTICK GLUE (round your answer up to the nearest whole number).**

The inventory record shown below for SURESTICK GLUE for the month of June has only been fully completed for the first three weeks of the month.

(b) **Complete the entries in the inventory record for the two receipts on 24 and 27 June that were ordered using the EOQ method.**

(c)   Complete ALL entries in the inventory record for the two issues in the month and for the closing balance at the end of June using the AVCO method of issuing inventory.

(Show the costs per litre in £'s to 3 decimal places; and the total costs in whole £'s, round up to nearest whole number).

Inventory record for SURESTICK GLUE

Date	Receipts			Issues			Balance	
	Quantity litres	Cost per litre (£)	Total cost (£)	Quantity litres	Cost per litre (£)	Total cost (£)	Quantity litres	Total cost (£)
Balance as at 23 June							65	130
24 June		2.234						
26 June				180				
27 June		2.341						
30 June				250				

(d)   Using the FIFO method, the issue of 180 kg to production on the 26 June would be valued at a total of _____.

6   GRAPE LTD

The inventory record shown below for glaze for the month of January has only been fully completed for the first three weeks of the month.

(a)   Identify the inventory valuation method used to complete the inventory record:

A   FIFO

B   AVCO

(b) **Complete ALL entries in the inventory record for the two issues in the month and identified in part (a).**

(Show the costs per drum in £'s to 3 decimal places; and the total costs in whole £'s).

Inventory record for glaze

Date	Receipts			Issues			Balance	
	Quantity drums	Cost per drum (£)	Total cost (£)	Quantity drums	Cost per drum (£)	Total cost (£)	Quantity drums	Total cost (£)
Balance as at 22 January							1,650	1,980
25 January	1,200	1.250					2,850	3,480
26 January				1,300		1,587		
28 January	1,200	1.302						
31 January				1,500				

(c) **Complete the following sentence with regard to FIFO as a method of pricing inventory.**

The FIFO method for costing issues **will/will not*** always mean that inventory is physically issued on a rotating basis so that the first inventory in is the first inventory issued.

7 **In a period of rising prices, which type of inventory valuation shows the highest profit?**

A   FIFO

B   AVCO

C   Neither

8 **In times of rising prices, the valuation of inventory using the First In First Out method, as opposed to the Weighted Average Cost method, will result in which ONE of the following combinations?**

	Cost of sales	Profit	Closing inventory
A	Lower	Higher	Higher
B	Lower	Higher	Lower
C	Higher	Lower	Higher
D	Higher	Higher	Lower

9   JUMP LTD

Jump Ltd had the following inventory of wooden poles:

Date purchased	Quantity	Cost per pole (£)	Total cost (£)
May 6	50	8.00	400
May 13	80	7.50	600
May 20	60	7.00	420

Jump Ltd issued 70 poles on the 25th May

(a)   Calculate the value of the issue and the balance after the issue using AVCO and FIFO (round to 4 decimal places for the cost per unit and round to the nearest pound for the final answer):

	Cost £
AVCO issue	
FIFO issue	
AVCO balance	
FIFO balance	

(b)   Which of the following costs would NEVER be included in Jump Ltd's inventory valuation?

    A   Prime costs

    B   Product costs

    C   Marginal costs

    D   Period costs

10   The following represent the materials transactions for a company for the month of December 20X6:

	£000s
Materials purchases	176
Issued to production	165
Materials written off	4
Returned to stores	9
Returned to suppliers	8

The material inventory at 1 December 20X6 was £15,000.

What is the closing balance on the materials inventory account at 31 December 20X6?

    A   £5,000

    B   £16,000

    C   £23,000

    D   £31,000

11 A number of transactions took place during October that need to be entered into the cost accounting records of Truck Transport Ltd.

The follow cost accounting codes are used:

Code	Description
2000	Bank
3000	PLCA
4000	Stores
5000	Maintenance
6000	General administration
8000	Direct costs
9000	Indirect costs

Identify the correct cost accounting entry for each of the following FOUR accounting transactions:

(a) **Return of 20 flap straps, costed at £50 each, from Maintenance to Stores.**

	Code	£
Debit		
Credit		

(b) **Payment to supplier for 15 padded steering wheels. These cost £75 each and were purchased on 30 day credit terms.**

	Code	£
Debit		
Credit		

(c) **Payment on receipt of a delivery of fuel costing £1,200.**

	Code	£
Debit		
Credit		

(d) **Issue of 300 litres of fuel at £1.23 to the short haul department.**

	Code	£
Debit		
Credit		

12 **The double entry for an issue of indirect production materials would be:**

A	Dr	Materials control account	Cr	Finished goods control account
B	Dr	Production overhead control a/c	Cr	Materials control account
C	Dr	Work-in-progress control account	Cr	Production overhead control a/c
D	Dr	Work-in-progress control account	Cr	Materials control account

LABOUR

13   CARTCYLE LTD

Below is a weekly timesheet for one of Cartcyle Ltd's employees, who are paid as follows:

- For a basic six-hour shift every day from Monday to Friday – basic pay.

- For any overtime in excess of the basic six hours, on any day from Monday to Friday – the extra hours are paid at time-and-a-half (basic pay plus an overtime premium equal to half of basic pay).

- For three contracted hours each Saturday morning – basic pay.

- For any hours in excess of three hours on Saturday – the extra hours are paid at double time (basic pay plus an overtime premium equal to basic pay).

- For any hours worked on Sunday – paid at double time (basic pay plus an overtime premium equal to basic pay).

Complete the columns headed Basic pay, Overtime premium and Total pay:

(**Notes:** Zero figures should be entered in cells where appropriate)

Employee's weekly timesheet for week ending 7 December

Employee:	A.Man		Profit centre:		Wood finishing	
Employee number:	C812		**Basic pay per hour:**		£8.00	
	Hours spent on production	Hours worked on indirect work	Notes	Basic pay £	Overtime premium £	Total pay £
Monday	6	2	10am – 12am cleaning of machinery			
Tuesday	2	4	9am – 1pm customer care course			
Wednesday	8					
Thursday	6					
Friday	6	1	3 – 4pm health and safety training			
Saturday	6					
Sunday	3					
Total	**37**	**7**				

14 A company employs a group of production workers who, as well as earning basic pay, are also paid a weekly group bonus based on their productivity during each week.

The group has a standard (target) output of 800 units of production per hour worked. All output in excess of this level earns a bonus for each of the employees.

The bonus % is calculated as:

$$25\% \times \frac{\text{Excess production (units)}}{\text{Standard production (units)}} \times 100$$

The bonus rate per hour is then calculated as: bonus % × £10.

The following information relates to this group's performance last week:

	Hours worked	Actual production (units)
Monday	920	940,000
Tuesday	870	890,000
Wednesday	910	930,000
Thursday	920	960,000
Friday	940	990,000
Saturday	440	690,000
Total	5,000	5,400,000

(a) **Use the table below to calculate the group bonus rate per hour and the total bonus to be paid to the group.**

	Units
Actual production	
Less standard production (based on actual hours worked)	
Excess production	
Bonus %	
Group bonus rate per hour £	
Total group bonus £	

(b) **An employee in this group worked for 44 hours last week, and is paid a basic rate of £9.60 per hour. The employee's total pay for last week was:**

£

15 GRAPES

Below is a weekly timesheet for one of Grape's employees, who are paid as follows:

- For a basic seven-hour shift every day from Monday to Friday – basic pay.

- For any overtime in excess of the basic seven hours, on any day from Monday to Friday – the extra hours are paid at basic pay plus an overtime premium is added of 50% of basic pay.

- For two contracted hours each Saturday morning – basic pay.

- For any hours in excess of two hours on Saturday – the overtime premium is paid at 75% of basic pay.

Complete the columns headed Basic pay, Overtime premium and Total pay:

(**Notes:** Zero figures should be entered in cells where appropriate)

Employee's weekly timesheet for week ending 31 January

Employee:		Olivia Michael	Profit centre:		Moulding Department	
Employee number:		P450	Basic pay per hour:		£10.00	
	Hours spent in work	Hours spent on indirect work	Notes	Basic pay £	Overtime premium £	Total pay £
Monday	8	3	10am – 1pm cleaning moulds			
Tuesday	7	4	9am – 1pm fire training			
Wednesday	8					
Thursday	7	1				
Friday	7	1	3 – 4pm annual appraisal			
Saturday	3					
Total	**40**	**9**				

Analyse the timesheet into production cost and production overhead costs.

Labour cost account

	£		£
Bank		Production	
		Production overheads	

16   Truck Transport Ltd employs a team of four mechanics who regularly service and valet the trucks.

The mechanics are paid a basic rate of £15.00 per hour and any overtime is paid at the following rates:

- Overtime rate 1: basic pay + 30%

- Overtime rate 2: basic pay + 50%

Truck transport sets a target for mechanics each month. A bonus equal to 75% of the basic hourly rate is payable for every service or valet in excess of the target.

The target for June for servicing was 50 trucks and 60 valets. The team completed 55 services and 63 valets.

All driving instructors work the same number of hours. Overtime premiums and bonuses are included as part of the indirect labour cost.

(a)   Complete the gaps in the table below to calculate the total labour cost for the mechanics.

Labour cost	Hours	£
Basic pay	620	
Overtime rate 1	36	
Overtime rate 2	20	
Total cost before bonus		
Bonus payment		
Total cost including bonus		

(b)   Calculate the direct labour cost per mechanic for June.

£

(c)   Complete the following sentence.

The total pay, including bonus, for each mechanic for June (to TWO decimal places) was:

£

and of this total, the bonus payable to each team member (to TWO decimal places) was:

£

17 A company operates a piecework system of remuneration. Employees must work for a minimum of 37 hours per week. Sebastian produces the following output for a particular week:

Product	Quantity	Standard time per item (hours)	Total actual time (hours)
Buckles	50	0.2	9
Press studs	200	0.06	14
Belts	100	0.1	12
Buttons	10	0.7	6
			——
			41
			——

Sebastian is paid £8.00 per standard hour worked. What are his earnings for the week?

A   £296

B   £302

C   £312

D   £328

18 Employees work in a team of 5 in the Wood painting department of Jump Ltd. They are paid a basic rate of £15 per hour, and any overtime is paid at the following rates:

- Overtime rate 1 – basic pay + 50%

- Overtime rate 2 – double pay

There is a target for painting wood each month and bonus of 10% of the basic hourly rate is paid for each pole painted in excess of the target.

The target for May was 3,000 poles and the team managed to paint 3,500 poles.

All the team members work the same number of hours and all overtime and bonuses are included as part of the direct labour cost.

(a)   **Complete the gaps in the table below to calculate the total labour cost for the team in May.**

Labour cost	Hours	£	Working
Basic pay	500		
Overtime rate 1	50		
Overtime rate 2	20		
Total cost before bonus	570		
Bonus			
Total cost including bonus			

(b)   **Calculate the total labour cost of painting a pole in May:**

(c)   **Complete the following sentences:**

The basic pay and overtime for each member of the team in May was £

The bonus payable to each team member was £

19   Information is available relating to the production of the tins of cat food for the month of July:

Total number of labour hours worked	10,800
Overtime hours worked	2,450
Standard hours for production in July	11,200
Normal rate per hour	£9
Overtime payment per hour	£14.50

The company operates a group incentive scheme, whereby a bonus of 35% of the normal hourly rate is paid for hours saved.

(a)   **Calculate the total cost of direct labour for July, assuming that overtime and the bonus are due to a specific customer request.**

Total basic pay (£)	
Total overtime premium (£)	
Hours saved (hours)	
Bonus (£)	
Total direct labour cost (£)	

(b)   In August the bonus was based on equivalent units. Employees will receive 45% of the basic hourly rate for every equivalent unit in excess of target. Rates of pay are not due to change in August. The target production is 450 units.

At the end of August 300 units were completed and there were 200 units of closing work in progress that was 100% complete for material and 75% complete for labour.

Calculate the number of equivalent units with regards to labour and the bonus payable.

Equivalent units	
Bonus (£)	

20 Below are extracts from Jump Ltd's payroll for last week

Date	Labour cost
6 May	Stores department Employees pay £1,500 + 10% bonus
11 May	Administration department Staff salaries £5,000 + 15% bonus
13 May	Wood trimming Production employees pay 600 hours at £8.50 per hour
15 May	Wood painting Production employees basic pay £5,500 + £300 overtime

The cost codes for the different accounts are:

Non-operating overheads	6000
Operating overheads	5000
Wages control account	4000
Wood painting direct costs	3021
Wood trimming direct costs	3022

Complete the cost journal entries to record the four payroll payments made in May

Date	Code	Dr £	Cr £
6 May			
6 May			
11 May			
11 May			
13 May			
13 May			
15 May			
15 May			

21 The payroll for maintenance employees for the week ending 30 November has been completed. The following payments are to be made:

	£
Net wages/salaries to pay to employees	10,000
Income tax and national insurance contributions (NIC) to pay to HMRC	2,000
Pension contributions to pay to F4L pension scheme	1,000
Gross payroll costs	13,000

The payroll for the week is analysed as:

	£
Direct labour costs	7,000
Indirect labour costs	4,000
Maintenance administration labour costs	2,000
Gross payroll costs	13,000

The following cost account codes are used to record maintenance labour costs:

Code	Description
6200	Maintenance direct labour
6400	Maintenance overheads
6600	Maintenance administration
8200	Wages control

(a) **Complete the wages control account entries in the account shown below:**

Wages control account			
	£		£
Bank (net wages/salaries)		Maintenance (direct labour)	
HMRC (income tax and NIC)		Maintenance overheads	
Pension contributions		Maintenance administration	
	13,000		13,000

(b) **Complete the table below to show how the gross payroll cost for the week is charged to the various cost accounts of the business:**

Date	Code	Debit	Credit
30 November			
30 November			
30 November			
30 November			
30 November			
30 November			

22   A number of transactions took place during October that need to be entered into the cost accounting records of Truck Transport Ltd.

The follow cost accounting codes are used:

Code	Description
1000	Bank
4000	PLCA
5000	Stores
6000	Wages Control
7000	General administration
8000	Direct costs
9000	Indirect costs

Identify the correct cost accounting entry for each of the following FOUR accounting transactions:

(a)   **Payment of driver wages for the week amounting to 490 hours at £15.50 per hour.**

	Code	£
Debit		
Credit		

(b)   **Drivers worked 20 hours of overtime at time and a half at the specific request of a customer. How would the overtime premium be recorded in the accounts?**

	Code	£
Debit		
Credit		

(c)   **The stores supervisor monthly salary of £2,000.**

	Code	£
Debit		
Credit		

(d)   **Drivers worked 10 hours of overtime at time and a half due to general work pressures. How would the overtime premium be recorded in the accounts?**

	Code	£
Debit		
Credit		

JOB, BATCH AND SERVICE COSTING

23 A company operates a job costing system. Job 812 requires £60 of direct materials, £40 of direct labour and £20 of direct expenses. Direct labour is paid £8 per hour. Production overheads are absorbed at a rate of £16 per direct labour hour and non-production overheads are absorbed at a rate of 60% of prime cost.

What is the total cost of Job 812?

A £240

B £260

C £272

D £320

24 A business operates a batch costing system. The prime cost of a batch was £6,840 and it had used 156 direct labour hours. The fixed production overheads are absorbed on the basis of direct labour hours. The budgeted overhead absorption rate was based upon a budgeted fixed overhead of £300,000 and total budgeted direct labour hours of 60,000. The batch contained 500 items.

What is the cost per unit in the batch?

£

25 A hotel calculates a number of statistics including average cost per occupied bed per day.

The following information is provided for a 30-day period.

	Rooms with twin beds	Single rooms
Number of rooms in hotel	260	70
Number of rooms available to let	240	40
Average number of rooms occupied daily	200	30

Number of guests in period	6,450
Average length of stay	2 days
Payroll costs for period	£100,000
Cost of cleaning supplies in period	£5,000
Total cost of laundering in period	£22,500

The average cost per occupied bed per day for the period is:

A £9.90

B £9.88

C £7.20

D £8.17

26   Which of the following are features of service organisations?

(i)   High levels of inventory

(ii)   High proportion of fixed costs

(iii)   Difficulty in identifying suitable cost units

A   (i) and (ii) only

B   (i) and (iii) only

C   (ii) and (iii) only

D   All of these

ABSORPTION AND MARGINAL COSTING

27   Which of the following are true of marginal costing?

(i)   The marginal cost of a product includes an allowance for fixed production costs.

(ii)   The marginal cost of a product represents the additional cost of producing an extra unit.

(iii)   If the inventory increases over a year, the profits under absorption costing will be lower than with marginal costing.

A   (i) only

B   (ii) only

C   (ii) and (iii) only

D   (i), (ii) and (iii)

28   Which of these statements are true of marginal costing?

(i)   The contribution per unit will be constant if the sales volume increases.

(ii)   There is no under–or over–absorption of overheads.

(iii)   Marginal costing does not provide useful information for decision making.

A   (i) and (ii) only

B   (ii) and (iii) only

C   (ii) only

D   (i), (ii) and (iii)

29 The following information relates to a contract for transporting school children during May 20X7:

	£
Fuel and other variable overheads	9,200
Fixed costs:	
Drivers' wages, pension and national insurance	3,220
Other fixed overheads	23,000
Number of miles travelled	4,600

Calculate the cost per mile under:

(a) Marginal costing

£ [   ]

(b) Absorption costing

£ [   ]

30 Globe Ltd has prepared a forecast for the next quarter for Tomato fertilizer.

Globe budgets to produce 1,800kg of the fertiliser and sell 1,000kg. The cost and revenue for this budget is as follows:

	£000
Sales	50,000
Direct materials	7,560
Direct labour	17,640
Fixed production overheads	3,600
Advertising (fixed cost)	2,010

Globe has no opening inventory of the fertilizer.

Produce a marginal costing statement of profit or loss and an absorption costing statement of profit or loss:

Marginal costing	£000	£000
Sales		
Opening inventory		
Production costs		
Less: Closing inventory		
Less: Cost of sales		
Contribution		
Less: Fixed costs		
Profit for the period		

Absorption costing	£000	£000
Sales		
Opening inventory		
Production costs		
Less: Closing inventory		
Less: Cost of sales		
Gross profit		
Less: Non-production cost		
Profit for the period		

31 ILCB has the following information relating to one of its products:

- Selling price per unit   £12
- Prime cost per unit   £4
- Variable production overhead cost per unit   £3
- Budgeted fixed production overhead   £30,000 per month
- Budgeted production   15,000 units per month
- Budgeted sales   12,000 units per month
- Opening inventory   2,000 units

(a) **Produce a marginal costing statement of profit or loss.**

Marginal costing	£	£
Sales		
Opening inventory		
Production costs		
Less: Closing inventory		
Less: Cost of sales		
Contribution		
Less: Fixed costs		
Profit for the period		

(b) **What would the profit be under absorption costing principles?**

£

32   CPL is considering what the effect would be of costing its products under marginal costing principles, instead of under absorption costing principles that it currently follows:

The following information relates to one of the company's products:

Selling price per unit	£40
Prime cost per unit	£12
Variable production overhead cost per unit	£4
Budgeted fixed production overhead	£120,000 per month
Budgeted production	12,000 units per month
Budgeted sales	10,000 per month
Opening inventory	500 units

   (a)   **Calculate the contribution per unit:**

£

   (b)   **Calculate the profit per unit:**

£

   (c)   **Complete the table below to produce a statement of profit or loss for the product for the month under absorption costing principles.**

Absorption costing	£	£
Sales		
Opening inventory		
Production costs		
Less: Closing inventory		
Less: Cost of sales		
Gross profit		
Less: Non-production cost		
Profit for the period		

   (d)   **What would the profit be under marginal costing principles?**

£

33   A new company has set up a marginal costing system and has a budgeted profit for the period of £23,000 based on sales of 13,000 units and production of 15,000 units. This level of production represents the firm's expected long-term level of production. The company's budgeted fixed production costs are £3,000 for the period.

   If the company were to change to an absorption costing system the budgeted profit would be:

   A   £22,600

   B   £23,400

   C   £25,600

   D   £26,400

34   Jump Ltd is planning to launch a new painted pole. It will be manufactured in batches of 100.

The following cost estimates have been produced per batch of painted pole:

	£
Direct material	4,500
Direct labour	5,000
Variable production overheads	2,500
Fixed production overheads	1,750
Administration, selling and distribution costs	2,250

(a)   **Calculate the estimated prime cost per batch of painted poles.**

£

(b)   **Calculate the estimated marginal production cost per batch of painted poles.**

£

(c)   **Calculate the estimated full absorption cost of one batch of painted poles.**

£

ATTRIBUTING COSTS

OVERHEADS

35   **At the end of a period, in an integrated cost and financial accounting system, the accounting entries for £10,000 overheads over-absorbed would be:**

A	Dr	Work-in-progress control account	Cr	Overhead control account
B	Dr	Statement of profit or loss	Cr	Work-in-progress control account
C	Dr	Statement of profit or loss	Cr	Overhead control account
D	Dr	Overhead control account	Cr	Statement of profit or loss

36   **During a period £50,000 was incurred for indirect labour. In a typical cost ledger, the double entry for this is:**

A	Dr	Wages control	Cr	Overhead control
B	Dr	WIP control	Cr	Wages control
C	Dr	Overhead control	Cr	Wages control
D	Dr	Wages control	Cr	WIP control

OVERHEAD ALLOCATION AND APPORTIONMENT

37   What is cost apportionment?

A   The charging of discrete identifiable items of cost to cost centres or cost units

B   The collection of costs attributable to cost centres and cost units using the costing methods, principles and techniques prescribed for a particular business entity

C   The process of establishing the costs of cost centres or cost units

D   The division of costs amongst two or more cost centres in proportion to the estimated benefit received, using a proxy, e.g. square feet

38   CARTCYLE LTD

Cartcyle Ltd's budgeted overheads for the next financial year are:

	£	£
Depreciation of plant and equipment		1,447,470
Power for production machinery		1,287,000
Rent and rates		188,100
Light and heat		41,580
Indirect labour costs:		
Maintenance	182,070	
Stores	64,890	
Administration	432,180	
Total indirect labour cost		679,140

The following information is also available:

Department	Carrying value of plant and equipment	Production machinery power usage (KwH)	Floor space (square metres)	Number of employees
Production:				
Wood cutting	10,080,000	3,861,000		25
Wood finishing	4,320,000	2,574,000		18
Support:				
Maintenance			25,200	9
Stores			15,120	3
Administration			10,080	12
Total	14,400,000	6,435,000	50,400	67

Overheads are allocated or apportioned on the most appropriate basis. The total overheads of the support cost centres are then reapportioned to the two production centres using the direct method.

- 70% of the Maintenance cost centre's time is spent maintaining production machinery in the Wood cutting production centre and the remainder in the Wood finishing production centre.

- The Stores cost centre makes 65% of its issues to the Wood cutting production centre, and 35% to the Wood finishing production centre.

- Administration supports the two production centres equally.

There is no reciprocal servicing between the three support cost centres.

Complete the overhead analysis table below:

	Basis	Wood cutting £	Wood finishing £	Maintenance £	Stores £	Admin £	Totals £
Depreciation of plant and equipment							
Power for production machinery							
Rent and rates							
Light and heat							
Indirect labour							
Totals							
Reapportion Maintenance							
Reapportion Stores							
Reapportion Admin							
Total overheads to production centres							

39 AQUARIUS

Aquarius Ltd calculates depreciation on a reducing balance basis, and allocates and apportions other overheads using the most appropriate basis for each

(a) **Complete the table below to identify a suitable basis for allocating or apportioning each overhead by selecting the most appropriate option.**

Overhead	Basis
Depreciation of plant and equipment	
Power for production machinery	
Rent and rates	
Light and heat	

Options:

- Carrying value of plant and equipment
- Production machinery power usage
- Floor space
- Indirect labour hours
- Number of employees

Aquarius has already allocated and apportioned its current costs for the next quarter, as shown in the table below. These costs have yet to be reapportioned to the two cost centres Assembly and Finishing.

The overhead allocated and apportioned to Administration is re-apportioned to the other production and support cost centres based on the number of employees. The number of employees is each department is:

Assembly 10, Finishing 10, Maintenance 6, Stores 4, Administration 8

The Stores cost centre makes 50% of its issues to the Assembly production centre, 30% to the Finishing production centre and 20% to Maintenance.

75% of the Maintenance cost centre's time is spent maintaining production machinery in the Assembly production centre and the remainder in the Finishing production centre.

(b) **Complete the table by reapportioning costs on the basis of the information given above. Enter your answers in whole pounds only. Indicate negative figures with minus signs, NOT brackets.**

	Assembly £	Finishing £	Maintenance £	Stores £	Admin £	Totals £
Depreciation of plant and equipment	420,000	280,000	–	–	–	700,000
Power for production machinery	403,000	217,000	–	–	–	620,000
Rent and rates	–	–	48,000	32,000	20,000	100,000
Light and heat	–	–	9,600	6,400	4,000	20,000
Indirect labour	–	–	102,000	40,000	240,000	382,000
Totals	**823,000**	**497,000**	**159,600**	**78,400**	**264,000**	**1,822,000**
Reapportion Admin						
Reapportion Stores						
Reapportion Maintenance						
Total overheads to production centres						

Another overhead is quality control costs. The estimated cost for the next quarter is £150,000, which consists of a fixed element and a variable element. The fixed element is 35% of the total cost and the rest is variable. The fixed element of the total cost is to be apportioned between the Assembly and Finishing departments in a ratio of 47:53. The variable element of the cost is apportioned in the ratio of 38:62.

(c)   Complete the following sentences by inserting the correct values.

The fixed element of the quality control costs that will be apportioned to the Assembly department is:

£

The variable element of the quality control costs that will be apportioned to the Finishing department is:

£

40   F4L

F4L has budgeted for the following overheads for its two profit and three cost centres for quarter 1 of the next financial year:

	£000	£000
Depreciation of aircraft		36,400
Aviation fuel and other variable costs		42,200
Pilots and aircrew salaries:		
Scheduled services	5,250	
Charter flights	4,709	
Total pilots and aircrew salaries		9,959
Rent and rates and other premises costs		12,600
Indirect labour costs:		
Aircraft maintenance and repairs	9,600	
Fuel and parts store	3,200	
General administration	7,800	
Total indirect labour cost		20,600

The following information is also available:

Profit/cost centre	Carrying amount of aircraft (£000)	Planned number of miles flown	Floor space (square metres)	Number of employees
Scheduled services	1,080,000	215,600		105
Charter flights	720,000	176,400		96
Aircraft maintenance and repairs			190,000	260
Fuel and parts store			114,000	146
General administration			76,000	220

Primary allocations or apportionments are made on the most appropriate basis. The support cost centres are then reapportioned to the two flight profit centres using the direct method.

- The Aircraft maintenance and repairs cost centre spends 60% of its time maintaining the aircraft in the scheduled services profit centre and the remainder in the charter flights profit centre.

- 55% of the issues from the Fuel and parts store cost centre are made to the scheduled services profit centre and the remainder to the charter flights profit centre.

- The scheduled services profit centre and the charter flights profit centre both incur general administration costs equally.

- The three support cost centres are not involved in reciprocal servicing.

Use the following table to allocate or apportion the overheads between the profit/cost centres, using the most appropriate basis.

	Basis	Scheduled services £000	Charter flights £000	Aircraft Maintenance £000	Fuel Stores £000	General Admin £000	Totals £000
Depreciation of aircraft							
Aviation fuel and other variables							
Pilots and aircrew salaries							
Rent and rates and other premises costs							
Indirect labour							
Totals							
Reapportion Maintenance							
Reapportion fuel stores							
Reapportion Gen Admin							
Total overheads to profit centres							

41   PREMIER LABELS LTD

Premier Labels Ltd produces labelled plastic food containers. The budgeted overheads for the next quarter are shown below, together with their behaviour and how they are apportioned to departments.

Budgeted cost	Cost behaviour	£	Comments
Heat and lighting	Semi-variable	60,000	Apportion fixed element of £24,000 equally between all four departments. Apportion variable element according to floor area.
Power for machinery	Variable	28,000	Apportion 70% to Plastics Moulding, and 30% to Labelling.
Supervision	Fixed	120,000	Apportion to the two production departments pro rata to direct labour costs.
Stores wages	Fixed	72,000	
Equipment Maintenance salaries	Fixed	188,200	
Depreciation of non-current assets	Fixed	84,000	Apportion according to carrying value of non-current assets.
Other overhead costs	Dependant on specific cost	128,000	Apportion 60% to Plastics Moulding, 20% to Labelling, and 10% each to Stores and Equipment Maintenance.

The following information is also available:

Department	Square metres occupied	Carrying value of non-current assets (£)	Number of material requisitions	Direct labour costs (£)
Plastics Moulding	320,000	160,000	162,750	100,000
Labelling	180,000	80,000	56,000	140,000
Stores	80,000	30,000		
Equipment Maintenance	20,000	10,000		

Notes: The Equipment Maintenance department's total costs should be apportioned equally to the other three departments. Then the total of the Stores department's costs should be apportioned according to the number of material requisitions.

Complete the overhead analysis table below:

	Basis	Plastics moulding £	Labelling £	Stores £	Equipment maintenance £	Totals £
Heat and lighting fixed cost						
Heat and lighting variable cost						
Power for machinery						
Supervision						
Stores wages						
Equipment maintenance salaries						
Depreciation of non-current assets						
Other overhead costs						
Totals						
Reapportion Maintenance						
Reapportion Stores						
Total overheads to production centres						

OVERHEAD ABSORPTION

42 **An overhead absorption rate is used to:**

A   share out common costs over benefiting cost centres

B   find the total overheads for a cost centre

C   charge overheads to products

D   control overheads

43   Cartcycle Ltd's budgeted overheads in the wood cutting department were £586,792. The overheads are absorbed based on machine hours. The budgeted machine hours were 9,464 and the actual machine hours were 9,745. The actual overhead cost was £568,631.

(a)   **What is the overhead absorption rate?**

    A   £62 per machine hour

    B   £60 per machine hour

    C   £58 per machine hour

    D   £55 per machine hour

(b)   **How much overhead was absorbed?**

    A   £584,700

    B   £586,768

    C   £604,190

    D   £565,210

(c)   **What is the under or over absorbed amount?**

    A   £35,559 over

    B   £35,599 under

    C   £21,582 over

    D   £21,582 under

44   Next quarter Aquarius Ltd's budgeted overheads and activity levels are:

	Assembly	Finishing
Budgeted overheads (£)	155,000	105,000
Budgeted direct labour hours	12,500	8,750
Budgeted machine hours	2,000	1,750

(a)   **What would the budgeted overhead absorption rate be for each department, if this were set based on their both being heavily automated?**

    A   Assembly £77.50/hour, Finishing £12/hour

    B   Assembly £77.50/hour, Finishing £60/hour

    C   Assembly £12.40/hour, Finishing £60/hour

    D   Assembly £12.40/hour, Finishing £12/hour

(b)   **What would the budgeted overhead absorption rate be for each department, if this were set based on their both being labour intensive?**

    A   Assembly £77.50/hour, Finishing £12/hour

    B   Assembly £77.50/hour, Finishing £60/hour

    C   Assembly £12.40/hour, Finishing £60/hour

    D   Assembly £12.40/hour, Finishing £12/hour

Additional data

At the end of the quarter actual overheads incurred in the finishing department were £119,000. Overheads were recovered on a machine hour basis. The machine hours worked were 10% less than budgeted.

(c)   **What was the under or over absorptions for finishing in the quarter?**

£ _____   under/over absorbed

45   **Next quarter Grape Limited's budgeted overheads and activity levels are:**

	Moulding Dept	Painting Dept
Budgeted overheads (£)	36,000	39,000
Budgeted direct labour hours	9,000	13,000
Budgeted machine hours	18,000	1,200

(a)   **What would the budgeted overhead absorption rate be for each department, if the most appropriate basis was chosen?**

A   Moulding £2/hour, Painting £32.50/hour

B   Moulding £32.50/hour, Painting £2/hour

C   Moulding £3/hour, Painting £33/hour

D   Moulding £2/hour, Painting £3/hour

Additional data

At the end of the quarter actual overheads incurred were found to be:

	Moulding Dept	Painting Dept
Actual overheads (£)	37,500	40,000
Actual direct labour hours	9,500	13,500
Actual machine hours	17,500	700

(b)   **How much overhead has been absorbed by each department?**

A   Moulding £35,000, Painting £40,500

B   Moulding £37,500 Painting £40,000

C   Moulding £19,000, Painting £2,100

D   Moulding £36,000, Painting £39,000

(c)   **Using your answer from b what are the under or over absorptions in the quarter?**

A   Moulding over absorbed £2,500, Painting over absorbed £500

B   Moulding under absorbed £2,500, Painting over absorbed £500

C   Moulding over absorbed £2,500, Painting under absorbed £500

D   Moulding under absorbed £2,500, Painting under absorbed £500

46 Next quarter Globe Limited's budgeted overheads and activity levels are:

	Mixing Dept	Bagging Dept
Budgeted overheads (£)	64,800	70,200
Budgeted direct labour hours	1,620	2,340
Actual direct labour hours	1,840	2,120
Budgeted machine hours	10,000	12,000
Actual machine hours	9,000	13,000

(a) What would the budgeted overhead absorption rate for each department, if the mixing department was heavily automated and the bagging department was labour intensive?

   A   Mixing £6.48/hour, Bagging £30.00/hour

   B   Mixing £7.20/hour, Bagging £33.11/hour

   C   Mixing £6.48/hour, Bagging £5.85/hour

   D   Mixing £5.00/hour, Bagging £5.00/hour

(b) How much overhead has been absorbed by production in each department?

   A   Mixing £13,248, Bagging £70,193

   B   Mixing £58,320, Bagging £76,050

   C   Mixing £58,320, Bagging £63,600

   D   Mixing £64,800, Bagging £70,200

Additional data

At the end of the quarter actual overheads incurred were found to be:

	Mixing Dept	Bagging Dept
Actual overheads (£)	67,500	75,600

(c) Using your answer from b what are the under or over absorptions in the quarter?

   A   Mixing under absorbed £9,180, Bagging over absorbed £12,000

   B   Mixing under absorbed £9,180, Bagging under absorbed £12,000

   C   Mixing over absorbed £9,180, Bagging over absorbed £12,000

   D   Mixing over absorbed £9,180, Bagging under absorbed £12,000

(d) Complete the following sentence (*delete as appropriate)

   An under absorption of overheads will be **debited/credited*** to the Profit and Loss account. This will **increase/decrease*** expenses and will **increase/decrease*** profit

47 **Over-absorbed overheads occur when:**

A   absorbed overheads exceed actual overheads

B   absorbed overheads exceed budgeted overheads

C   actual overheads exceed budgeted overheads

D   budgeted overheads exceed absorbed overheads

48 **The management accountant's report shows that fixed production overheads were over-absorbed in the last accounting period. The combination that is certain to lead to this situation is:**

A   production volume is lower than budget and actual expenditure is higher than budget

B   production volume is higher than budget and actual expenditure is higher than budget

C   production volume and actual cost are as budgeted

D   production volume is higher than budget and actual expenditure is lower than budget

ACTIVITY BASED COSTING

49 **The following statements have been made about ABC and cost drivers.**

(1)   A cost driver is any factor that causes a change in the cost of an activity.

(2)   For long-term variable overhead costs, the cost driver could be the volume of activity.

(3)   Traditional absorption costing tends to under-allocate overhead costs to low-volume products.

Which of the above statements is/are true?

A   (1) and (3) only

B   (2) and (3) only

C   (1) and (2) only

D   (1), (2) and (3)

50 The following statements have been made in relation to activity-based costing:

(1)   A cost driver is a factor which causes a change in the cost of an activity.

(2)   Traditional absorption costing tends to under-estimate overhead costs for high-volume products.

Which of the above statements is/are true?

A   (1) only

B   (2) only

C   Neither (1) nor (2)

D   Both (1) and (2)

51 The ABC Company manufactures two products, Product Alpha and Product Beta. Both are produced in a very labour-intensive environment and use similar processes. Alpha and Beta differ by volume. Beta is a high-volume product, while Alpha is a low-volume product. Details of product inputs, outputs and the costs of activities are as follows:

	Direct labour hours/unit	Annual output (units)	Number of purchase orders	Number of set-ups
Alpha	5	1,200	70	40
Beta	5	10,800	80	60
			150	100

Fixed overhead costs amount to a total of £420,000 and have been analysed as follows:

	£
Labour-related	90,000
Purchasing related	150,000
Set-up related	180,000

(a) **Using a traditional method of overhead absorption based on labour hours, what is the overhead cost per unit for each unit of product Alpha?**

   A   £7.00

   B   £24.91

   C   £35.00

   D   £125.83

(b) **Using a traditional method of overhead absorption based on labour hours, what is the overhead cost per unit for each unit of product Beta?**

   A   £7.00

   B   £24.91

   C   £35.00

   D   £125.83

(c) **Using Activity Based Costing as method of overhead absorption, what is the overhead cost per unit for each unit of product Alpha?**

   A   £7.00

   B   £24.91

   C   £35.00

   D   £125.83

(d) **Using Activity Based Costing as method of overhead absorption, what is the overhead cost per unit for each unit of product Beta?**

   A   £7.00

   B   £24.91

   C   £35.00

   D   £125.83

52 A company uses activity-based costing to calculate the unit cost of its products. The figures for Period 3 are as follows: production set-up costs are £84,000. Total production is 40,000 units of each of products A and B, and each run is 2,000 units of A or 5,000 units of B.

What is the set-up cost per unit of B?

A   £0.10

B   £0.08

C   £0.60

D   £0.29

53   DOG

Details of four products and relevant information are given below for one period:

Product	W	X	Y	Z
Output in units	240	200	160	240
Costs per unit	£	£	£	£
Direct material	80	100	60	120
Direct labour	56	42	28	42
Machine hours (per unit)	8	6	4	6

The production overhead is currently absorbed by using a machine hour rate, and the total of the production overhead for the period has been analysed as follows:

	£
Machine department costs	20,800
Set up costs	10,500
Stores receiving	7,200
Total	38,500

You have ascertained that the 'cost drivers' to be used are as listed below for the overhead costs shown:

Cost	Cost driver
Machine department costs	Machine hours
Set up costs	Number of production runs
Stores receiving	Requisitions raised

The four products are similar and are usually produced in production runs of 40 units.

The number of requisitions raised on the stores was 40 for each product.

Calculate the total cost and the cost per unit for each product, using activity based costing:

Total costs	W	X	Y	Z
	£	£	£	£
Direct materials				
Direct labour				
Machine department costs				
Set up costs				
Stores receiving				
Total cost				
Cost per unit				

SHORT TERM DECISION MAKING

COST BEHAVIOURS

54   The following data relate to two output levels of a department:

Machine hours	17,000	18,500
Overheads	£246,500	£251,750

The amount of fixed overheads is:

A   £5,250

B   £59,500

C   £187,000

D   £246,500

55   A manufacturing company has four types of cost (identified as T1, T2, T3 and T4).

The total cost for each type at two different production levels is:

Cost type	Total cost for 125 units	Total cost for 180 units
T1	£	£
T1	1,000	1,260
T2	1,750	2,520
T3	2,475	2,826
T4	3,225	4,644

Which two cost types would be classified as being semi-variable?

A   T1 and T3

B   T1 and T4

C   T2 and T3

D   T2 and T4

56 The following eight options describe the behaviour of different types of costs during a short period of one quarter of a year.

Option	Description	Option	Description
1	Decreases per unit as volume increases	5	Fixed for a certain volume range only
2	Increases per unit as selling price increases	6	Made up of fixed and variable costs
3	Variable for a certain volume range only	7	Increase in total as volume increases
4	Decreases in total as volume increases	8	Decreases per unit as selling price increases

What is the correct description for the following four types of cost?

	Description
Variable cost	
Fixed cost	
Stepped cost	
Semi-variable cost	

57 **Identify the TWO types of cost behaviour shown below:**

Graph 1   **Graph 2**

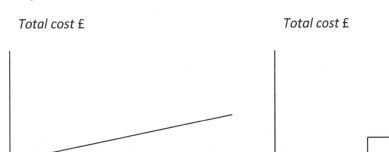

A Variable   A Variable

B Fixed   B Fixed

C Semi variable   C Semi variable

D Stepped fixed   D Stepped fixed

58   TRUCK TRANSPORT

Truck Transport Ltd is reviewing costs for the next month for contract Route NW. The cost analysis table below shows cost behaviour per miles travelled for four different cost classifications.

	Cost per mile travelled			
	1,500 miles	3,000 miles	4,500 miles	6,000 miles
Cost 1	14.00	7.00	6.00	4.50
Cost 2	7.00	7.00	7.00	7.00
Cost 3	21.00	10.50	7.00	5.25
Cost 4	12.00	9.00	8.00	7.50

Complete the table below by:

(a)   selecting the correct classification for each cost

(b)   calculating the total cost at 5,000 miles travelled for each cost.

Cost	Classification (tick correct answer)				Total cost at 5,000 miles (£)
	Variable	Semi-variable	Fixed	Stepped fixed	
Cost 1					
Cost 2					
Cost 3					
Cost 4					

59   CARTCYCLE LTD

Cartcyle Ltd has prepared a forecast for the next quarter for one of its wooden products, DR43. This component is produced in batches and the forecast is based on selling and producing 2,160 batches.

One of the customers of Cartcyle Ltd has indicated that it may be significantly increasing its order level for product DR43 for the next quarter and it appears that activity levels of 2,700 batches and 3,600 batches are feasible.

The semi-variable costs should be calculated using the high-low method. If 5,400 batches are sold the total semi-variable cost will be £13,284, and there is a constant unit variable cost up to this volume.

Complete the table below and calculate the estimated profit per batch of DR43 at the different activity levels.

Batches produced and sold	2,160	2,700	3,600
	£	£	£
Sales revenue	64,800		
Variable costs:			
• Direct materials	9,720		
• Direct labour	22,680		
• Overheads	12,960		
Semi-variable costs:	6,804		
• Variable element			
• Fixed element			
Total cost	52,164		
Total profit	12,636		
Profit per batch (to 2 decimal places)	5.85		

60 CHARTER FLIGHTS

Charter Flights profit centre has just revised its forecasts for the number of miles it expects to fly during the next month on a particular charter contract. Originally it expected the contract would be for flights totalling 5,000 miles. Charter Flights now expects that the total miles to be flown will increase to either 6,000 or 7,000 miles.

Notes:

- The company chartering the flights has negotiated with Charter Flights a reduction of 10% per mile, paid on all miles flown in excess of the 5,000 miles agreed in the original contract.

- Landing and servicing fees are a semi-variable cost. There is a fixed charge of £600,000 plus £50/mile.

Complete the table below and calculate the estimated profit per mile flown at the different activity levels.

Likely miles	5,000	6,000	7,000
	£000	£000	£000
Sale revenue	2,500		
Variable/semi-variable costs:			
• Aviation fuel	400		
• Landing and servicing fees	850		
• Other variable overheads	135		
Fixed costs:			
• Wages and salaries	420		
• Other fixed overheads	625		
Total cost	2430		
Total profit	70		
Profit per mile flown (2 decimal places) £	14.00		

61 Grape Ltd is negotiating a new contract with a customer for one of its products – The Owl. Owl is produced in batches and the forecast is based on selling and producing 800 batches.

The customer has indicated that it may be increasing its order level for Owl for the next quarter and it appears that activity levels of 1,200 units and 1,500 units are feasible.

The semi-variable costs should be calculated using the high-low method. If 1,600 batches are sold the total semi-variable cost will be £4,920, and there is a constant unit variable cost up to this volume.

Revenues and costs for 800 Owls are shown below. Fixed costs remain constant through the range being considered.

Units produced and sold	800
	£
Sales revenue	24,000
Variable costs:	
• Direct materials	3,600
• Direct labour	8,400
• Overheads	1,800
Semi-variable costs	2,520
Total cost	16,320
Total profit	7,680
Profit per batch (to 2 decimal places)	9.60

Calculate the following:

(a)   The sales revenue per unit if the contract is for 800 Owls

(b)   The variable cost per unit if the contract is for 1,200 Owls

(c)   The fixed cost per unit if the contract is for 1,200 Owls

(d)   The total cost per unit if the contract is for 1,500 Owls

(e)   The profit per unit if the contract is for 1,500 Owls

SEGMENTAL REPORTS

62   Truck Transport Ltd is planning new routes for the next month, Route S, Route SE and Route SW. The following data has been put together for the routes.

1   The contract for Route S is for 3,000 miles and the rate is £150 per mile

The contract for Route SE is for 20% less miles that Route S with a rate of 10% more.

The contract for Route SW is for 20% more miles that Route S with a rate of 10% less.

2   Variable costs are £80 per mile for Route S

Variable costs are £5 more per mile for Route SE than Route S

Variable costs are 6.25% less per mile for Route SW than Route S

3   The fixed costs for the contracts will total £400,000 to be apportioned 20% to Route S, 30% to Route SE and the remainder to Route SW.

(a)   You are required to complete the following table to show the forecast contribution and profit for the three new routes.

	Route S	Route SE	Route SW
Contract miles			
Revenue and costs			
Revenue (£000s)			
Variable costs (£000s)			
Contribution (£000)			
Fixed costs (£000)			
Profit (£000s)			

63 INDIA LTD

India Ltd manufactures and sells three ranges of pottery, Rose, Tulip and Buttercup. The following information has been provided for the next quarter.

	Rose	Tulip	Buttercup
Sales revenue (£)	50,000	24,000	40,000
Direct materials (£)	10,000	4,800	8,000
Direct labour (£)	13,000	8,800	10,500

India Ltd expects to produce and sell 1,000 units of Rose and 200 units of Tulip. The budgeted sales demand for Buttercup is 50% less than that of Rose. Budgeted total fixed costs are £52,000.

Complete the table below (to two decimal places) to show the budgeted contribution per unit for the three products and the company's budgeted profit or loss for the year.

	Rose (£)	Tulip (£)	Buttercup (£)	Total (£)
Selling price per unit				
Less: Variable costs per units				
Direct material				
Direct labour				
Contribution per unit				
Sales volume (units)				
Total contribution				
Less: fixed costs				
Budgeted profit/loss				

64 SPORT SHIRT LTD

Sport Shirts Ltd has provided the following cost and sales information for a new range and an existing range of sports shirts:

	New	Existing
Sales and production units	2,000	3,000
Labour hours per month	500	1,500
Unit selling price	£12.00	£20.00
Unit material cost	£3.75	£4.00
Unit direct labour cost	£1.25	£2.50

The company expects its monthly fixed costs to be as follows:

- Production   £11,400
- Sales   £12,100
- Administration   £10,250

(a) Complete the table below to calculate the forecast total monthly contribution and total profit for the company from the sale and production of both shirt ranges.

	New £	Existing £	Total £
Sales revenue			
Less: variable costs			
Direct materials			
Direct labour			
Total contribution			
Less: fixed costs			
Budgeted profit/loss			

COST VOLUME PROFIT ANALYSIS

65 Choose the correct description for each of the following:

Term
Contribution
Breakeven point
Margin of safety

Description
Excess of actual sales over breakeven sales
Selling price less variable costs
Sales units where is no profit or loss

66 Cartcycle Ltd has the following budgeted costs per unit for product MR13:

		£
Variable costs	Direct material	7.50
	Direct labour	8.00
	Overheads	11.50
Total variable costs		27.00
Fixed costs	Overheads	7.20
Total costs		34.20

Product MR13 has a selling price of £41.40 per unit. Budgeted sales volume is 9,000 units.

(a) Calculate the budgeted fixed overheads for product MR13.

£

(b) Calculate the budgeted breakeven volume, in units, for product MR13.

units

(c)   Complete the table below to show the budgeted margin of safety in units and the margin of safety percentage if Cartcyle Ltd sells 9,000 units of product MR13.

Units of MR13 sold	9,000
Margin of safety (units)	
Margin of safety percentage (2dp)	

(d)   If Cartcyle Ltd increases the selling price of MR13 by £1.80 what will be the impact on the breakeven point and the margin of safety assuming no change in the number of units sold?

A   The breakeven point will decrease and the margin of safety will increase

B   The breakeven point will stay the same but the margin of safety will decrease

C   The breakeven point will decrease and the margin of safety will stay the same

D   The breakeven point will increase and the margin of safety will decrease

Cartcycle Ltd wishes to make a profit of £36,000 on the sale of MR13.

(e)   Complete the table below to calculate the number of units that Cartcycle Ltd must sell to achieve its target profit, the margin of safety (%) and the margin of safety in sales revenue for the target profit assuming that the sales demand, selling price and all costs remain as per budget.

	Product MR13
Number of units to be sold to meet target profit	
Revised margin of safety to 2 decimal places (%)	
Revised margin of safety in sales revenue (£)	

67   Seafood soup sells for 80p per can. It has a marginal cost of production of 30p per can. Fixed costs attributable to this range of soups total £312,500.

(a)   Calculate the sales revenue of seafood soup CCS has to achieve to break even.

£

(b)   Calculate the sales revenue of seafood soup CCS needs to achieve to make a profit of £200,000.

£

(c)   If CCS were to sell £875,000 worth of seafood soup, what would be:

(i)   the margin of safety

£

(ii)   the margin of safety percentage over the break-even sales?

%

68 The following budgeted annual sales and cost information relates to labelled food containers types A and B:

Product	A	B
Units made and sold	300,000	500,000
Machine hours required	60,000	40,000
Sales revenue (£)	450,000	600,000
Direct materials (£)	60,000	125,000
Direct labour (£)	36,000	70,000
Variable overheads (£)	45,000	95,000

Total fixed costs attributable to A and B are budgeted to be £264,020.

(a) Complete the table below (to 2 decimal places) to show the budgeted contribution per unit of A and B sold, and the company's budgeted profit or loss for the year from these two products.

	A (£)	B (£)	Total (£)
Selling price per unit			
Less: variable costs per unit			
Direct materials			
Direct labour			
Variable overheads			
Contribution per unit			
Sales volume (units)			
Total contribution			
Less: fixed costs			
Budgeted profit or loss			

The £264,020 of fixed costs attributed to products A and B can be split between the two products: £158,620 to A and £105,400 to B.

The latest sales forecast is that 250,000 units of product A and 400,000 units of product B will be sold during the year.

(b) Using your calculations and the additional data above, complete the table below to calculate:

Product	A	B
Fixed costs (£)		
Unit contribution (£)		
Break-even sales (units)		
Forecast sales (units)		
Margin of safety (units)		
Margin of safety (%)		

(c) Which of the 2 products has the safer margin of safety?

Product A		Product B	

69 Eastern Bus Company (ECB) has produced three forecasts of miles to be driven during the next three months for a particular contract. The original contract is for journeys totalling 10,000 miles. It now seems likely, however, that the total journeys involved will increase to either 12,000 or 14,000 miles.

(a) Complete the table below in order to estimate the profit per mile (in pounds, to 3 decimal places) of this contract for the three likely mileages.

Likely miles	10,000	12,000	14,000
	£	£	£
Sales revenue	100,000		
Variable costs:			
• Fuel	8,000		
• Drivers' wages and associated costs	5,000		
• Overheads	6,000		
Fixed costs:			
• Indirect labour	10,600		
• Overheads	25,850		
Total cost	55,450		
Total profit	44,550		
Profit per mile	4.455		

(b) Using the information provided above and your own calculations for that task, calculate:

Forecast number of miles		12,000	14,000
Sales revenue	£		
Fixed costs	£		
Contribution	£		
Contribution per mile	£		
Break-even number of miles	Miles		
Break-even sales revenue	£		
Margin of safety in number of miles	Miles		
Margin of safety in sales revenue	£		
Margin of safety	%		

70 Four lines representing expected costs and revenues have been drawn on a breakeven chart:

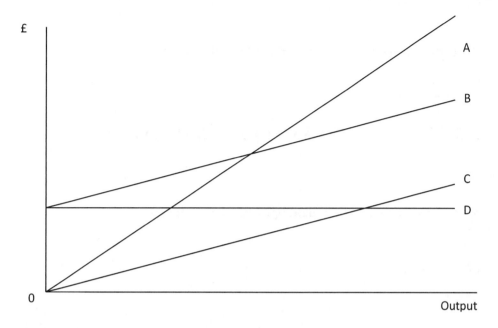

Match the line letter with the correct description?

A
B
C
D

Fixed costs
Total revenue
Total costs
Total variable costs

71 Jump Ltd manufactures wooden poles. One length (0.8m) of pole is produced in batches of 150 poles. Each pole is sold for £10. The following are the costs involved in its manufacture:

Batch of 150 0.8m poles	£
Direct material	75
Direct labour	200
Variable overheads	250
Fixed overheads	325

(a) **Calculate the breakeven volume of 0.8m poles:**

(b) **Calculate the breakeven sales revenue of 0.8m poles.**

Jump Ltd also manufactures 2.8m poles. This is manufactured in batches of 50 poles and makes a contribution of £1,500 per batch. Fixed costs are £450. Jump Ltd has set a target profit of £2,400 from manufacture and selling this pole.

(c) How many 2.8m poles must Jump sell to reach its target profit of £2,400.

```
┌──────────────────────────┐
│                          │
└──────────────────────────┘
```

(d) Calculate the margin of safety of the 2.8m pole (in poles).

```
┌──────────────────────────┐
│                          │
└──────────────────────────┘
```

PRINCIPLES OF BUDGETING AND CASH MANAGEMENT

BUDGETING

72 **What are the main purposes of budgeting? (tick all that apply)**

to give authority to spend	
to control expenditure	
to aid decision making.	

73 **Which of the following is NOT a purpose of budgeting?**

A   Planning

B   Co-ordination

C   Consultation

D   Communication

74 **Which two of the following are not characteristics of rolling budgets?**

	Characteristic of rolling budgets?
Budgets are more likely to be realistic as there is a shorter period between preparation and actual events occurring	
Updates to budgets are only made when they are foreseeable	
They reduce uncertainty in budgeting	
They force management to look ahead more frequently	
Each item of expenditure must be fully justified before inclusion in the budget	

75   What is a flexible budget?

A   a budget for semi-variable overhead costs only

B   a budget which, by recognising different cost behaviour patterns, is designed to change as volume of activity changes

C   a budget for a twelve month period which includes planned revenues, expenses, assets and liabilities

D   a budget which is prepared for a rolling period which is reviewed monthly, and updated accordingly

76   Which of the following statements are correct? (tick all that apply)

A fixed budget is a budget that considers all of an organisation's costs and revenues for a single level of activity.	
A flexible budget is a budget that is produced during the budget period to recognise the effects of any changes in prices and methods of operation that have occurred.	
Organisations can use budgets to communicate objectives to their managers.	

77   East manufactures a single product which has the following specification:

Raw materials – 5 kg @ £7.50 per kg

Direct labour – 2 hours @ £7.50 per hour

Variable overheads – 2 hours @ £2 per hour

Fixed overheads – 2 hours @ £5 per hour

Complete the standard cost card using absorption costing principles.

	£ per unit
Raw material	
Labour	
Variable overhead	
Fixed overhead	
Standard cost for one unit	

CASH MANAGEMENT

78   Which of the following items would affect a company's cash flow but not its profits:

A   Payment of salaries to directors

B   Payment of interest on a loan

C   Depreciation of a motor vehicle

D   Money raised from a new share issue

79 Identify whether the following items affect cash, profit, or both cash and profit.

Item	Cash	Profit	Cash and profit
Depreciation			
Selling a non-current asset for its carry value			
Repaying a loan			
Prepaying next year's rent			
Making a cash sale			

80 Which one of the following is the main function of liquidity management?

A   keeping cash in the bank

B   making a profit

C   meeting any liabilities due

D   investing in capital expenditure

81 Why is liquidity management important?

A   Liquidity management is important to ensure that a company does not make a loss.

B   Liquidity management is important so that the shareholders can see how much return they will get on their investment.

C   Liquidity management is important so that the company can estimate how much cash is tied up in inventory and non-current assets.

D   Liquidity management is important so that the company can ensure that cash is available to discharge commitments.

82 Extracts from a company's accounts show the following balances:

	£000		£000
Inventories	150	Revenue	2,700
Receivables	300	Cost of sales	1,300
Cash	25	Gross profit	1,400
Payables	230	Admin costs	500
Overdraft	90	Distribution costs	350
		Operating profit	550
		Finance cost	75

(a)   What is the trade receivables' collection period in days (to the nearest day)?

A   41 days

B   84 days

C   78 days

D   45 days

(b)   What is the trade payables' payment period in days (to the nearest day)?

A   31 days

B   65 days

C   60 days

D   35 days

(c)   What is the inventory holding period (to the nearest day)?

A   4 days

B   10 days

C   24 days

D   42 days

(d)   What is the working capital cycle?

A   18 days

B   23 days

C   64 days

D   66 days

83   A company has provided the following information:

Trade receivables collection period	38 days
Raw material inventory holding period	8 days
Production period (WIP)	4 days
Trade payables payment period	28 days
Finished goods holding period	26 days

The working capital cycle for the business is _____ days.

84   GH has gathered the following information for the year ended 30 June 20X2.

	30 June 20X2
Gross profit	500,000
Trade receivables	145,000
Trade payables	95,000
Trade receivables collection period in days	22
Inventory holding period in days	47

(a)   **Complete the table below (round to the nearest whole £)**

	30 June 20X2
Sales revenue	
Cost of sales	
Inventories level in the statement of financial position	
Trade payables payment period in whole days	

(b)   **The cash operating cycle for GH is** [   ] **days**

---

85 A company has an overdraft facility of £5,000 and has the following forecast cash balances:

	January	February	March	April	May	June
Opening cash balance £	4,000	10,000	16,000	-2,000	-5,000	2,000
Closing cash balance £	10,000	16,000	-2,000	-5,000	2,000	10,000

(a) In what month will the company go into its overdraft?

(b) In what month will the company need to raise further capital as it has exceeded its overdraft limit?

86 Identify whether the following actions should have a positive or negative impact on the cash flow of a business in the short term.

Action	Positive	Negative
Delay paying suppliers		
Extend the credit terms currently offered to customers		
Offer credit to new customers		
Reduce the credit terms currently offered to customers		
Extending credit terms with suppliers		
Paying suppliers on receipt of an invoice		
Increasing credit limits to existing customers		

PREPARTION OF BUDGETS

87 A company has a budget, for two products A and B, as follows:

	Product A	Product B
Sales (units)	1,000	2,250
Production (units)	875	2,500
Labour:		
Skilled at £12/hour	1.5 hours/unit	1 hours/unit
Unskilled at £8/hour	2.5 hours/unit	2 hours/unit

Calculate the total labour cost to be included in the budget.

88 A job requires 1,350 standard labour hours for completion but it is anticipated that idle time will be 10% of the total time budgeted. If the wage rate is £7 per hour, what is the budgeted labour cost for the job, including the cost of the idle time?

A £8,505

B £9,450

C £10,395

D £10,500

89 The following items were extracted from a company's budget for next month:

	£
Purchases on credit	180,000
Expected increase in trade payables during the month	7,500

What is the budgeted payment to trade payables for the month?

A   £166,500

B   £172,500

C   £178,500

D   £187,500

90 The following items are included in a company's budget for next month:

	£
Sales on credit	120,000
Expected decrease in trade receivables next month	6,000

What is the budgeted receipt from trade receivables next month?

91 V is preparing a cash budget for July. The credit sales are as follows.

	£
April	20,000
May	15,000
June	10,000
July	12,500

His recent debt collection experience has been as follows.

Current month's sales	20%
Prior month's sales	60%
Sales two months prior	10%
Irrecoverable debts	5%

How much may V expect to collect from credit customers during July?

A   £9,000

B   £10,000

C   £10,500

D   £12,000

92   EVA pays its suppliers on the basis of 20% one month after date of purchase, 50% two months after purchase and the remainder three months after the date of purchase.

The trade payables are forecast to be:

	£
January	2,570
February	2,000
March	2,500

Complete the table below to identify how much EVA would expect to pay to its payables in April.

April	£

93   Which of the following would NOT be included in a cash budget? (tick all that apply)

Depreciation	✓
Provisions for doubtful debts	✓
Wages and salaries	

BUDGETS AND DEVIATIONS

VARIANCE ANALYSIS

94   **Which of the following statements are correct? (tick all that apply)**

An adverse variance increases profit	
A favourable variance increases profit	
A favourable variance will arise when actual revenue is greater than budgeted revenue	
An adverse variance will arise when actual costs are greater than budgeted costs	

95   A company manufactures a single product but activity levels vary widely from month to month. The budgeted figures are based on an average activity level of 10,000 units of production.

The actual figures for last month for production of 9,500 units are also shown:

	Budget £	Actual £
Direct labour	10,000	9,400
Materials	5,000	4,800
Variable overhead	5,000	4,300
Depreciation	10,000	10,000
Fixed overhead	5,000	5,200
	35,000	33,700

(a)   Calculate the variable overhead variance for the month and state if it is adverse or favourable. £_____ adverse/favourable

(b)   Calculate the fixed overhead variance for the month and state if it is adverse or favourable. £_____ adverse/favourable

96   AQUARIUS LTD

Aquarius Ltd. has the following original budget and actual performance for product Britz for the year ending 31 December.

	Budget	Actual
Volume sold	200,000	267,000
	£000	£000
Sales revenue	1,600	2,409
Less costs:		
Direct materials	400	801
Direct labour	200	267
Fixed overheads	600	750
Profit from operations	400	591

Complete the table below to show a flexed budget and the resulting variances against this budget for the year. Show the actual variance amount, for sales and each cost, in the column headed 'Variance' and indicate whether this is Favourable or Adverse by entering F or A in the final column. If neither F nor A enter 0.

	Flexed budget	Actual	Variance	Favourable (F) or Adverse (A)
Volume sold		267,000		
	£000	£000	£000	
Sales revenue		2,409		
Less costs:				
Direct materials		801		
Direct labour		267		
Fixed overheads		750		
Profit from operations		591		

97   GRAPE LTD

Grape Ltd. has the following original budget and actual performance for product Bird Box Sets for the year ending 31 December.

(a)   Complete the table below to show a flexed budget and the resulting variances against the budget for the year. Show the actual variance amount, for sales and each cost, in the column headed 'Variance'.

Note:

- Adverse variances must be denoted with a minus sign or brackets

- Enter 0 where any figure is zero.

	Original budget	Flexed budget	Actual	Variance
Volume sold	20,000		28,800	
	£000	£000	£000	£000
Sales revenue	3,000		3,877	
Less costs:				
Direct materials	175		212	
Direct labour	875		912	
Variable overheads	445		448	
Fixed overheads	300		325	
Profit from operations	1,205		1,980	

(b)   Referring to your answer for part (a), which one of the following has had the greatest impact in increasing the profit from operations?

A   Sales revenue

B   Direct materials

C   Direct labour

D   Variable overheads

(c)   Which of the following might have caused the variance for direct labour?

A   An increase in units produced

B   An increase in employees' pay

C   Improved efficiency of employees

D   An increase in overtime

98   GLOBE LTD

Globe Ltd. has the following original budget and actual performance for product Bean for the year ending 31 December.

(a)   **Complete the table below to show a flexed budget and the resulting variances against the budget for the year. Show the actual variance amount, for sales and each cost, in the column headed 'Variance'.**

Note:

- **Adverse variances must be denoted with a minus sign or brackets**

- **Enter 0 where any figure is zero.**

	Original budget	Flexed budget	Actual	Variance
Volume sold	4,000		5,000	
	£000	£000	£000	£000
Sales revenue	1,500		1,950	
Less costs:				
Direct materials	36		45	
Direct labour	176		182	
Variable overheads	92		90	
Profit from operations	1,196		1,633	

(b)   **Referring to your answer for part (a), which one of the following has had the least impact in increasing the profit from operations?**

A   Sales revenue

B   Direct materials

C   Direct labour

D   Variable overheads

(c)   **Which of the following might have caused the variance for sales revenue?**

A   An increase in units produced

B   Offering a bulk discount

C   Increased competition from other companies

D   An increase in selling price

SPREADSHEETS FOR MANAGEMENT ACCOUNTS

SPREADSHEETS

99 **In the Excel spreadsheet below, what is the name given to cell B6?**

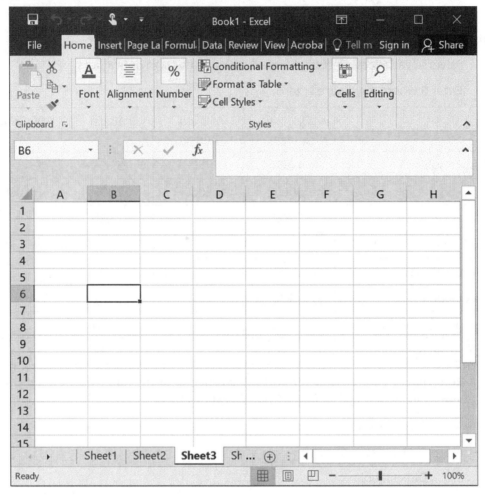

A   work cell

B   current cell

C   active cell

D   key cell

100 You prepare a budget using a spreadsheet program. The numerical data is presented in a tabular form. However, the tabulated data can also be presented in alternative or additional forms.

Which of the following methods of data presentation CANNOT be produced automatically by a spreadsheet programme?

A   Bar chart

B   Narrative (words)

C   Pie chart

D   Graph

101 The following statements relate to spreadsheets:

(i)   A spreadsheet consists of records and files.

(ii)   Most spreadsheets have a facility to allow data within them to be displayed graphically.

(iii)   A spreadsheet could be used to prepare a budgeted statement of profit or loss.

(iv)   A spreadsheet is the most suitable software for storing large volumes of data.

Which of the above statements are correct?

A   (i) and (ii) only

B   (i), (iii) and (iv) only

C   (ii) and (iii) only

D   (iii) and (iv) only

102 **Which of the following are benefits of using spreadsheet software?**

(i)   Variety

(ii)   Speed

(iii)   Accuracy

(iv)   Legibility

A   All of them

B   (ii), (iii) and (iv) only

C   (ii) and (iii) only

D   (i) and (iv) only

103 The following spreadsheet shows an extract from a company's cash flow forecast.

	A	B	C	D	E
1	**Cash flow forecast**				
2					
3			Jan	Feb	March
4	**Inflows**				
5	Cash sales		10,000	12,000	11,500
6	Cash from debtors		24,500	26,200	15,630
7	Disposal of non-current assets		0	0	12,000
8	Other		10	0	0
9	**Total inflows**		**34,510**	**38,200**	**39,130**

Which of the following formulae will generate the correct figure for cell D9?

A   SUM(D5:D8)

B   SUM(D5;D8)

C   =SUM(D5:D8)

D   =SUM(D5;D8)

104 In 'Format cells, Number, Percentage', what will figure 0.25 be shown as?

A 0.25

B 0.25%

C 25.00

D 25.00%

105 If cell B3 contains the value 10.567 and cell B4 contains the formula '=ROUND(B3,0)', what would be the value in cell B4?

A 11

B 10.6

C 10.57

D 10.567

106 To make a cell address absolute .i.e. to always use the contents of that cell, which ONE of the following symbols should be used?

A £

B $

C %

D *

107 A salesman receives a basic salary and a bonus based on 5% of sales made. His/her basic salary is entered on to a spreadsheet in cell B5. His/her sales figure is split between 'home' sales in cell C5 and 'overseas' sales in cell D5. The commission percentage of 5% is entered in cell E5.

Which formula in cell F5 would be used to determine the total commission?

A =(C5 + D5)*E5

B C5+D5*E5

C (C5+D5)*E5

D =C5+D5*E5

108 In cell B2 an accountant enters the number of hours employees usually work per week, which is 40 hours. In cells C10 to C14 the employees' actual hours worked are entered. They range from 38 to 42 hours dependent on the employee. In cells D10 to D14 the accountant wishes to note whether the employee will receive overtime, by using an IF function.

Which formula should be held in cell D10 so it can be copied to D11 through to D14?

A   =IF(C$10>B2,"OVERTIME","N/A")

B   =IF(C10>B2,"OVERTIME","N/A")

C   =IF(C10>$B2,"OVERTIME","N/A")

D   =IF(C10>B2,"OVERTIME","N/A")

109 The data below is not arranged in any order.

	A	B	C	D	E
1	Supplier	Quantity	Price(£)	Value(£)	Rank
2	X	10	2.00	20	
3	Z	125	0.50	48	
4	W	100	0.48	48	
5	Y	10	4.00	40	

To SORT the Price (£) into descending order you should start by:

A   Selecting the data range A2:C5> Data> Sort, choose to sort Column C

B   Selecting the data range A2:C5> Data, choose to sort Column C> Sort

C   Selecting the data range C2:C5> Data> Sort> choose to sort Column C

D   Selecting the data range C2:C5> Sort> Data, choose to sort Column C

110 **Which of the following is the correct syntax for a ROUND function?**

A   Round(number,digits)

B   Round(digits,number)

C   Round(number,digits,0)

D   Round(digits,number,0)

111 **Under which menu is the option to include graphs and charts found in Microsoft Excel 2016?**

A   Formulas

B   Page Layout

C   View

D   Insert

The excel workbooks needed for the following questions can be found within your MATS course on MyKaplan.

Please go to www.mykaplan.co.uk and login using your username and password.

SPREADSHEETS, BUDGETING AND CASH MANAGEMENT

112 Pretty Things is a small manufacturing company that makes curtains, which are sold online on a three different websites.

The Production Manager wants you to prepare a spreadsheet workbook that will help with budgeting.

On the 'Budget' worksheet:

(a) In cells B13:B15 insert a formula to calculate the total cost per pair of curtains. Use a function to round the cost up to two decimal places.

(b) Your manager wants to make 20% profit on each pair of curtains. Use a formula to calculate the selling price per pair of curtains in cells C13:C15. Use to function to round to the nearest £.

(c) In cells D13:D15 use a formula to calculate the profit per pair of curtains.

(d) In cells E13:E15 calculate the total profit based on the budgeted sales volumes for each design of curtain. In cell E16 calculate the total profit for the budgeted sales.

(e) Use an IF function in cell E18 that confirms the total profit is 20% or more of the total cost. The cell should say "yes" if it 20% or more and "no" if it is less than 20%

On the 'Sales distribution' worksheet:

(g) In cell I1 insert a pivot table that show the number of each type of curtain sold by each retailer.

(h) Insert a clustered column chart to show the sales of each curtain design split by the retailer

On the 'Forecast' worksheet:

Your manager wants to calculate the future possible sales amounts for the Tropical and the Adriana curtain

(i) Use the Forecast function to predict the sales for months 9 to 12 (cells B10:B13 and C10:C13) for the Adriana and Tropical curtains. Round the answers down to the nearest pair of curtains.

(j) Produce a scatter graph for months 1 to 12 with lines of best fit showing the trend on the sales for each type of curtain. Make the Adriana trend line blue and the Tropical trend line red. Move the chart to a new sheet

113 CARA is a soft furnishing manufacturer and produces round and square cushions. They are developing their budget for 20X8. The plan is to increase sales volume by 15% on 20X7 figures.

On the budget worksheet:

(a)   In cells B4 and C4 use a formula to calculate the planned level of sales for 20X8.

The sales director would like to increase the selling price by 3%.

(b)   In cells B5 and C5 use a formula to calculate the total revenue CARA should hope to receive. Use a formula to round your answer to the nearest whole £.

Quantities of the two materials per unit is not due to change but the cost of the material will decrease by 10% due to the availability of bulk discounts.

(c)   In cells B8:C9, use Vlookups to calculate the total quantity for each product for each type of material. In D8:D9 calculate the total material requirements.

(d)   In cells E8 and E9 use Vlookups to calculate the total cost of each material.

(e)   Use formulas to calculate the labour costs for each product in cells B12:E13.

CARA's is assuming that the revenue will incur evenly over the year and that sales receipts are split into 40% cash sales, 30% 1 month after sale and the remainder 2 months after sale.

CARA assumed that purchases will occur evenly over the year and they pay the material suppliers 40% one month after receiving the goods and the rest two months after.

The monthly wages are paid in the month of production.

(f)   On the Cash worksheet enter the cash receipts and cash payments for January to June. Link the figures from the budget worksheet and using formulas and the information on the budget worksheet complete cells B5:G10, B15:G20.

(g)   In cells B24:G26 use conditional formatting to highlight any negative figures in red text.

114 CT Ltd is investigating its cash management procedures and the finance manager has provided you with some data in a spreadsheet but some of the data is missing.

On the 'Data' worksheet

(a)   Using a formula calculate the cost of sales in cell B8.

(b)   Using a formula and function, calculate the Trade receivables collection period in days in cell B12 rounded to 2 decimal places

(c)   Using a formula and function, calculate the Inventory levels cell B4, round to the nearest whole £.

(d)   Using a formula calculate the Working capital cycle in days in cell B15

On the 'cash budget' worksheet

(e)   Use formulae in rows 7 and 15 to calculate the total receipts and total payments for each month.

(f)   In row 17 use formulae to calculate the net cash flow for each month.

(g)   In row 19 use formulae to calculate the closing balance for each month

(h)   In row 18 use formulae to calculate the opening balance for each month.

If the previous months closing cash balance is overdrawn CT will be charged 0.5% interest in the current month.

(i)   In row 14 use an IF statement to calculate the interest.

(j)   In row 19 apply conditional formatting to highlight any cells in black with white font where CT is overdrawn.

(k)   In cell A21 insert the title Maximum overdraft and in cell B21 use a function to show the largest amount the overdraft is over the year (based on the closing cash balance)

The finance manager would like to know what the opening balance in January would need to be to prevent CT Ltd from going into its overdraft.

(l)   Using What-if analysis make the value of the maximum overdraft zero by changing the opening balance in January. **Before** clicking OK take a screen shot of the goal seek screen and paste it into a blank worksheet. Rename the blank worksheet What-if.

(m)   Protect the 'Cash budget' worksheet, leave the password blank.

SPREADSHEETS, BUDGETS AND DEVIATIONS

115   Elf Ltd is wanting to compare the original budget and actual performance for one of its products, The Reindeer, for the last December. Each Reindeer sells for £65.00. Elf Ltd had planned to sell 2,500 last December but actually sold 2,750.

On the 'Cost card' worksheet

(a)   Use formulae to complete the 'Cost per Reindeer' column

On the 'Variances' worksheet

(b)   Use the information above to complete the budgeted sales revenue in cell B4

(c)   Use a Vlookup to complete the Budgeted costs in cells B6:B9, Elf Ltd absorbs fixed overheads based on the number of units produced.

(d)   Use a formula to calculate the budgeted profit in cell B10

(e)   Calculate the flexed budget sales revenue in cell C4

(e)   Use a Vlookup to complete the flexed budgeted costs (where applicable) in cells C6:C9

(f)   In cells E4 and E6:E10 calculate the variances in £ using appropriate formula, indicate an adverse variance with a minus sign

(g)   Format values B4:E10 to number, zero decimal places, and thousands separator.

Your manager would like to be informed of any significant variances. A significant variance is one that is adverse and more than 4% of budget.

(g)   In cells F4 and F6:F9 calculate the variance as a percentage of the flexed budget using appropriate formulae and format to two decimal places

(h)   Use an IF statement to say 'investigate' if the variance is significant and adverse, the cell should stay blank if investigation is not required

116 Ziggy Ltd makes boxes in different shapes and you have been provided with some data on the costs associated with producing the boxes.

On the 'Data' worksheet

(a)   Use the Subtotal function to insert a subtotal at each change in cost element which sums the cost (£000)

(b)   Copy the worksheet and paste it into a blank worksheet, remove the subtotals. Call the new worksheet 'Pivot'.

On the 'Pivot' worksheet

(c)   Insert a pivot table that show the total cost for each cost element over the six months January to June. Add the Product as a filter.

(d)   Insert a clustered column chart. Apply suitable filter(s) to your graph to show your manager the figures for only direct labour each month.

Your manager would like to compare the actual results with the budgeted results.

On the 'Variance' worksheet

(e)   Copy and paste values the totals for each cost element from the 'Data' worksheet into the cells D10:D12 in the 'Variance' worksheet

(f)   In cell D1 enter a formula to use to flex the fixed budget

(g)   Flex the budget (as applicable) in cells C8 and C10:C13

(h)   In cells E8:E13 use formulas to calculate the variances. Format the font so that the adverse variances show in red with a minus sign.

(i)   Format the values in the other cells to number, zero decimal place and thousands separator.

117 Echo Ltd has produced its variance analysis for the first quarter of 20X1 but the budget data has gone missing.

On the 'Variances' worksheet

(a)   Using formulae and the information available on the worksheet calculate the flexed budget values.

(b)   Using formulae and the information available on the worksheet calculate the original budget values.

(c)   In cells F8 and F10:F13 calculate the variance percentage of budget using an appropriate formula, round the values to the nearest whole number.

Your manager would like to be informed of any significant variances. A significant variance is any variance that is 5% or more of budget

(d)   Use conditional formatting to highlight any significant variances in column F for your manager. The cells should be filled in red.

(e)   In cells G8 and G10:G13 use an IF and AND statement to say 'Investigate' if the variance is significant, the cell should stay blank if investigation is not required

Your manager would like to see how the total cost is split over the different costs in the budget

(f)   Produce a column chart that shows the variance percentages. Remove the Axis labels and add data labels to the end of each column to show what the revenue or cost type the columns refer to. Add a title to the graph. Turn the adverse variance columns red and the favourable variance columns green

SCENARIOS

These following scenarios are more expansive than you would find in your exam but allow you to practice using excel in detail.

118   Slick Partz

You are an Accounting Technician working for the UK Branch of a company called Slick Partz. Your branch is a franchise of the parent company which is based in Europe. Slick Partz manufactures parts for hospital equipment at its factory in main land Europe and these are then sold to franchisees. The franchise is then responsible for selling the parts to hospitals in its sales area.

The franchise buys the parts from the parent company in Euros (€) but sells to the hospitals in GB Pounds (£).

Required:

TASK 1

On 'Sheet 1' worksheet:

(a)   In Column D format the Cost Price data as currency. It should be formatted as € Euros (€ 123) to 2 decimal places.

(b)   In Columns E and F format the Cost Price and Sale Price data as currency. It should be formatted to GB Pounds to 2 decimal places.

(c)   Rename Sheet 1 as 'Data'.

(d)   Copy the 'Data' worksheet to a new worksheet in the same workbook and name it as 'Subtotals'.

(e)   Go back to the 'Data' worksheet and set the page orientation to portrait and fit the data to the width of one page.

(f)   Save the workbook as 'Slick Partz'.

TASK 2

On the 'Subtotals' worksheet:

(a)   Sort the data before carrying out subtotalling. The subtotals that are needed are for Model and Salesperson.

(b)   Create subtotals for Model, summing the Sales quantity.

(c)   Create a further subtotal for Salesperson, summing the Sales quantity.

(d)   Convert the worksheet to show formulas.

(e)   Set the page orientation to landscape.

(f)   Save the workbook.

TASK 3

On a new worksheet:

(a)   Name the new worksheet 'Currency Conversion'.

(b)   Return to the 'Data' worksheet and Auto-Filter the data.

(c)   Filter by sales person 'Monty Video'.

(d)   Copy the result and paste it into Cell A1 in the currency conversion worksheet.

(e)   Return to the Data worksheet and remove the 'Monty Video' filter.

(f)   Save the workbook.

TASK 4

On the 'Currency Conversion' worksheet:

(a)   Insert 3 rows at the top of the worksheet.

(b)   In Cell D1, type 'Conversion Rate' and make the font bold and underline the text. Format D1 to Right Justified.

(c)   Format Cell E1 to number to 2 decimal places and type 0.84.

(d)   Make the font bold in cells A4:I4.

(e)   In Cell E5:E26 create a formula that converts the content of Cell D5:D26 to GBP (£) by multiplying by the conversion rate in Cell E1. Use absolute referencing where necessary.

(f)   The sales price is 20% more than the cost price £. In cells F5:F26 use a formula to calculate the sales price.

(g)   Copy cells A4:I26 from the 'Currency conversion' worksheet and paste special, to include the values and number formatting, into a new worksheet and rename the new worksheet as 'Profit Calculation'.

(h)   Return to the 'Currency conversion' worksheet and show formulas. Auto fit the column widths.

(i)   Set the page orientation to landscape.

(j)   Save the workbook.

TASK 5

On the 'Profit Calculation' worksheet:

(a)   In Cells J1, K1 and L1 create 3 new headings of 'Total Cost', 'Total Revenue' and 'Profit'. Make all the column heading bold.

(b)   In Cell J2:J23 create a formula that calculates the total cost.

(c)   In Cell K2:K23 create a formula that calculates the total revenue.

(d)   In Cell L2:L23 create a formula that calculates profit.

(e)   In Cells J25:L25 use a function to calculate the average cost, average revenue and the average profit. Add the heading 'Averages' in cell I25.

(f)   In Cells J26:L26 use a function to calculate the largest number in each of the data sets. Add the heading 'Largest' in cell I26.

(g)   In Cells J27:L27 use a function to calculate the smallest number in each of the data sets. Add the heading 'Smallest' in cell I27.

(h)   Show formulas and auto-fit column widths.

(i)   Set the page orientation to landscape, and move the page break to the left of column I.

(j)   Save the workbook.

TASK 6

On the 'Data' worksheet:

(a)   Using the data create a Pivot Table in a new worksheet that shows the quantity of each individual model sold by each salesperson. The model should be the columns and the salesperson the rows.

(b)   Rename the worksheet 'Pivot' and move it to the right of the 'Profit Calculation' sheet.

(c)   Remove Grand Totals for Rows and Columns.

(d)   Create a Pivot Chart and locate it on the Pivot worksheet. The type of chart should be a Clustered Column Chart. Add the title 'Sales Quantity' to the chart.

(e)   Add Customer as a Filter.

(f)   Save the workbook.

TASK 7

On a new worksheet:

(a)   Name the new worksheet 'Product Lookup'.

(b)   In cell A2 type 'Product Code', in cell A6 type 'Inventory levels' and in cell A9 type 'Sales quantity'. Fit the contents to the cell.

(c)   In cell B2 create a list of product codes from the 'Data' worksheet using Data Validation. Pick the product code WM4369.

(d)   In cell B6 create a VLOOKUP to look up the product code in Cell B2 in the 'Data' worksheet and return the quantity. The VLOOKUP should be set to look for only exact matches.

(e)   In cell B9 create a VLOOKUP to look up the product code in Cell B2 in the 'Data' worksheet and return the sales quantity. The VLOOKUP should be set to look for only exact matches.

(f)   In Cell B12, use an IF function that produces the word "Re-order" if the value in Cell B9 is greater than the value in Cell B6 but leaves it blank if not.

(g)   In cell C12, use an IF function that calculates the difference between the inventory levels and the sales quantity if "Re-order" appears in B12 but leaves it blank if not.

(h)   Set page orientation to landscape.

(i)   Save the workbook.

119 Crazy Cars

You work as a payroll assistant for a car sales company called Crazy Cars.

Required:

TASK 1

On the 'Employee Information' worksheet:

(a)   Place the TODAY function in Cell B10.

(b)   In column C use a formula to calculate the number of days each employee has worked for Crazy Cars with reference to the TODAY function in Cell B10. Use absolute and relative referencing where appropriate. Change the format of these cells to general so the number of days is shown rather than the date.

(c)   In column D use a function to convert the number of days into years, rounding down to the nearest whole year.

(d)   Show formulas and auto-fit column widths.

(e)   Save your work as 'Crazy Cars'.

TASK 2

On the 'Basic Pay' worksheet:

The basic wage is dependent on the number of full years each employee has worked for the business.

An employee's starting rate (for the first 12 months) is £160 per week.

The basic rate per week increases by 10% for each full year of employment up to a maximum of 5 years.

(a)   Using the information above calculate the weekly pay for an employee at the company based on 0 to 25 years of employment.

(b)   Format the basic wage to pounds and pence.

(c)   Save your work.

TASK 3

The sales team are paid a basic wage plus commission for the cars that they sell.

Each employee receives 5% of the profit they have earned from each car they have sold that week.

Any cars sold at a loss must be highlighted for the Finance Manager.

On the 'Car Sales Information' worksheet:

(a)　In column E use a formula to calculate the profit (sales less cost) made for each vehicle. Add a suitable title in cell E1.

(b)　Using an IF function, in column F calculate the amount of commission earned on each vehicle. If the car has been sold at a loss, then "none" should appear in the cell. Add a suitable title in cell F1.

(c)　All monetary values should be formatted to currency (£) to 2 decimal places.

(d)　In column E use conditional formatting to identify the value of any losses. The cell fill should turn red.

(e)　Auto-fit column widths.

(f)　Save your work.

TASK 4

Using the 'Car Sales Information' worksheet:

(a)　Create a pivot table in a new worksheet that shows the total commission earned by each salesperson (columns) per make of car (rows).

(b)　Format the values in the pivot table as currency £ to 2 decimal places.

(c)　Name the pivot table worksheet as 'Pivot'.

(d)　Move the 'Pivot' worksheet to the right of the 'Car Sales Information' worksheet.

(e)　Save your work.

TASK 5

On the 'Total Pay' worksheet:

(a)　Show the following information:

　(ii)　In column B, use a VLOOKUP from the 'Employee Information' worksheet to extract the number of years each employee has been employed.

　(iii)　In column C, use a VLOOKUP from the 'Basic Pay' worksheet, to calculate the applicable basic weekly pay for each employee.

　(iv)　In column D, use a HLOOKUP from the 'Pivot' worksheet, enter the commission earned per employee.

　(v)　In cell D10 use a function to determine the average commission earned.

　(vi)　Any member of staff who earns more than the average commission each week receives an extra £100 bonus. In column E use an IF statement that calculate any bonus.

　(vii)　In column F, using the Sum function – calculate the total pay for each employee for the week and the total wages the company is paying that week.

　(viii)　Format all monetary amounts to pounds and pence.

　(ix)　Show formulas and auto-fit column widths.

(b)　Save your work.

TASK 6

The Finance Director wants to see how each sales person has contributed to the total commission earned.

(a)   Create a pie chart using the 'Total Pay' worksheet to show each employees commission as a proportion of the total commission.

(b)   Give the pie chart a suitable title and add percentage labels to the chart.

(c)   Move the pie chart to a new worksheet called 'Pie chart' and move the sheet to the right of the 'Total Pay' worksheet.

(d)   Save your work.

120   Goodtime Travel

Goodtime Travel is a firm of Travel Agents that specialises in long haul package holidays. It buys the flights and hotel rooms in bulk from the airlines and hotels. It is a reputable firm and gets most of its custom from customers who have used its service before.

Required:

TASK 1

Customers can receive discounts off their holidays. A discount will only be given if a customer has booked a previous holiday with Goodtime Travel. A discount is given of 2p per mile flown on the previous holiday.

This discount is then deducted from the price of the current holiday. However, the Finance Director is considering adapting the discount rates so that they are different for each destination. Details of the miles travelled for each destination are given on the Discounts worksheet.

On the 'Discounts' worksheet:

(a)   In Column C use a formula to calculate the discount for a particular destination, use absolute referencing where appropriate.

(b)   Format the discount column as currency (£) to 2 decimal places.

(c)   Show formulas and auto-fit column widths.

On the 'Weekly Sales' worksheet:

(d)   In the Discount column (column F) use a VLOOKUP from the 'Discounts' worksheet to calculate any applicable discounts.

(e)   In the column G, use a formula to calculate the amount owing for each booking deducting any discounts for repeat customers.

(f)   Format the values to £ currency to 2 decimal places in columns F and G.

(g)   Set the orientation to landscape and fit the data to one page.

(h)   Save the workbook as 'Goodtime Travel'.

TASK 2

Goodtime Travel has recently invested in a marketing campaign to try and encourage new customers to use its service. The Marketing Manager has said that the campaign will be viewed as a success if at least 40% of income each week is generated from new customers.

On the 'Weekly sales' worksheet:

(a)   Create a pivot table in a new worksheet to show how much revenue has been generated from new customers compared to existing customers (columns) for the different destinations (rows).

(b)   Call this worksheet 'Pivot' and move it to the right of the 'Weekly sales' worksheet.

(c)   In cell G15 on the 'Pivot' worksheet create an expression to calculate the total % of income generated from new customers. The answer should be formatted as percentage and 2 decimal places. In cell F15 add the title "% new customers" and fit the content to the cell.

(d)   In cell H15 use an IF function for the Marketing Director to determine whether the campaign was a success. "Successful" should appear if more than 40% of the income is generated from new customers and "Unsuccessful" if less than 40% of the income is generated from new customers. Format the outcome of the IF formula by making it bold, and enlarging the text to font size 16.

(e)   Save the workbook.

TASK 3

The Finance Director is considering changing the discount on offer per mile for repeat customers. He/she wants the discount amounts for the following destinations changed to:

Destination	New Discount	Currently
Sydney	£250.00	£424.00
Fiji	£300.00	£404.36

On the 'What If Analysis' worksheet:

(a)   Copy all the discount information from the 'Discount' worksheet and paste it into the 'What if Analysis' worksheet.

(b)   Using What If Analysis – Goal Seek, calculate what the revised discount rate per mile needs to be to reduce the discount offered for Sydney. Copy and 'paste–special values' the result to cell D20. Provide a suitable heading in A20. Reset the original discount rate per mile to 2p.

(c)   Using What If Analysis – Goal Seek, calculate what the revised discount rate per mile needs to be to reduce the discount offered for Fiji. Copy and 'paste–special values' the result to cell D22. Provide a suitable heading in A22. Reset the original discount rate per mile to 2p.

(d)   Show formulas, auto-fit column width and save your work.

(e)   Save the workbook.

Section 2

ANSWERS TO PRACTICE QUESTIONS

COST TECHNIQUES

MATERIALS

1   A

The EOQ formula is $\sqrt{\dfrac{2 \times \text{cost of ordering} \times \text{annual demand}}{\text{Cost of holding one unit for one year}}}$

2   A

The cost of placing an order includes administrative costs, postage and quality control costs.

3   GLOBE LTD

(a)   Re-order level = (1,500 + 3,500)/2 × (2 + 4)/2 + 17,000 = 24,500 components

(b)   Maximum inventory = 17,000 + 15,750 = 32,750 components

(c)   Minimum re-order quantity = 2,500 × 3 = 7,500 components

4   PLASTIC

(a)

The EOQ $\sqrt{\dfrac{2 \times 3.60 \times 112.500}{1.80}} = 671$

(b)   Inventory record card

Date	Receipts			Issues			Balance	
	Quantity kgs	Cost per kg (£)	Total cost (£)	Quantity kgs	Cost per kg (p)	Total cost (£)	Quantity kgs	Total cost (£)
Balance as at 22 July							198	238
24 July	671	2.336	1,567				869	1,805
26 July				540	1.920	1,037	329	768
28 July	671	2.344	1,573				1,000	2,341
30 July				710	2.341	1,662	290	679

Workings:

Issue on 26th July is made up of 198 @ 1.202 and 342 @ 2.336

Issue on 30th July is made up of 329 @ 2.336 and 381 @ 2.344

5   SURESTICK GLUE

(a)   The EOQ = $\sqrt{\dfrac{2 \times 2.50 \times 2,500 \times 12}{1.00}}$ = 388

(b)   Inventory record card

Date	Receipts			Issues			Balance	
	Quantity litres	Cost per litre	Total cost (£)	Quantity litres	Cost per litre	Total cost (£)	Quantity litres	Total cost (£)
Balance as at 23 June							65	130
24 June	388	2.234	867				453	997
26 June				180	2.201	397	273	600
27 June	388	2.341	909				661	1,509
30 June				250	2.283	571	411	938

(c)   £130 + (115 × £2.234) = **£387**

6   GRAPE LTD

(a)   B – AVCO

(b)   Inventory record card

	Receipts			Issues			Balance	
Date	Drums	Cost per Drum (£)	Total cost (£)	Drums	Cost per drum (p)	Total cost (£)	Drums	Total cost (£)
Balance as at 22 January							1,650	1,980
25 January	1,200	1.250	1,500				2,850	3,480
26 January				1,300	1.221	1,587	1,550	1,893
28 January	1,200	1.302	1,562				2,750	3,455
31 January				1,500	1.256	1,884	1,250	1,571

(c)   The FIFO method for costing issues **will not** always mean that inventory is physically issued on a rotating basis so that the first inventory in is the first inventory issued.

7   A – FIFO

8   A

When prices are rising, FIFO will give a higher valuation for closing inventory, because the closing inventory will consist of the most recently-purchased items. Higher closing inventory means lower cost of sales and higher profit.

9   (a)

	Cost £	Workings
AVCO issue	523	(400 + 600 + 420) ÷ (50 + 80 + 60) = 7.4737 70 × 7.4737 = 523
FIFO issue	550	400 + (20 × 7.50) = 550
AVCO balance	897	(400 + 600 + 420) – 523 = 897
FIFO balance	870	(400 + 600 + 420) – 550 = 870

(b)   D

10   C

Materials inventory account

	£000s		£000s
Opening inventory	15	Issued to production	165
Payables for purchases	176	Returned to suppliers	8
Returned to stores	9	Written off	4
		Closing balance (balancing item)	23
	_____		_____
	200		200
	_____		_____

11

(a)   **Return of 20 flap straps, costed at £50 each, from Maintenance to Stores.**

	Code	£
Debit	4000	1,000
Credit	5000	1,000

(b)   **Payment to supplier for 15 padded steering wheels. These cost £75 each and were purchased on 30 day credit terms.**

	Code	£
Debit	3000	1,125
Credit	2000	1,125

(c)   **Payment on receipt of a delivery of fuel costing £1,200.**

	Code	£
Debit	4000	1,200
Credit	2000	1,200

(d)   **Issue of 300 litres of fuel at £1.23 to the short haul department.**

	Code	£
Debit	8000	369
Credit	4000	369

12   B

Indirect materials are overhead costs so debit production overhead. An issue of materials is a credit from the material control account.

LABOUR

13   CARTCYLE LTD

Employee's weekly timesheet for week ending 7 December

Employee:		A. Man		Profit centre:		Wood finishing	
Employee number:		C812		**Basic pay per hour:**	£8.00		
	Hours spent on production	Hours worked on indirect work	Notes		Basic pay £	Overtime premium £	Total pay £
Monday	6	2	10am – 12am cleaning of machinery		64	8	72
Tuesday	2	4	9am – 1pm customer care course		48	0	48
Wednesday	8				64	8	72
Thursday	6				48	0	48
Friday	6	1	3 – 4pm health and safety training		56	4	60
Saturday	6				48	24	72
Sunday	3				24	24	48
Total	**37**	**7**			352	68	420

Alternative

Sunday	3				0	48	48
Total	**37**	**7**			328	92	420

14   (a)

	Units
Actual production	5,400,000
Standard production (5,000 hours at 800 units)	(4,000,000)
Excess production	1,400,000
Bonus %	$\dfrac{25\% \times 1,400,000}{4,000.000} = 8.75\%$
Group bonus rate per hour	0.0875 × £10 = £0.875
Total group bonus	5,000 hours at £0.875 = £4,375

(b) Basic pay 44 hours at £9.60 =   £422.40

Bonus pay 44 hours at £0.875 =   £38.50

_____

Total pay   £460.90

15   GRAPES

Employee's weekly timesheet for week ending 31 January

Employee:		Olivia Michael	Profit centre:			Moulding Department	
Employee number:		P450	Basic pay per hour:			£10.00	
	Hours spent in work	Hours worked on indirect work	Notes	Basic pay £	Overtime premium £	Total pay £	
Monday	8	3	10am – 1pm cleaning moulds	80	5	85.00	
Tuesday	7	4	9am – 1pm fire training	70	0	70.00	
Wednesday	8			80	5	85.00	
Thursday	7	1		70	0	70.00	
Friday	7	1	3 – 4pm annual appraisal	70	0	70.00	
Saturday	3			30	7.50	37.50	
Total	**40**	**9**		400	17.50	417.50	

Labour cost account

	£			£
Bank	417.50		Production	310
			Production Overheads	107.50

Production is direct labour only therefore basic hours less time spent on non-production activities:

$(40 - 9) \times £10 = £310$

Production overheads are the indirect costs therefore the cost is:

$£17.50 + (9 \times £10) = £107.50$

16 **(a)** Complete the gaps in the table below to calculate the total labour cost for the mechanics.

Labour cost	Hours	£
Basic pay	620	620 × 15 = 9,300
Overtime rate 1	36	36 × (15 × 1.3) = 702
Overtime rate 2	20	20 × (15 × 1.5) = 450
Total cost before bonus		10,452
Bonus payment		(5 + 3) × 15 × 0.75 = 90
Total cost including bonus		10,542

(b) Calculate the direct labour cost per mechanic for May.

(620 + 36 + 20) × 15 = £10,140/4 = £2,535

(c) Complete the following sentence.

The total pay, including bonus, for each mechanic for June (to TWO decimal places) was:

£10,542/4 = £2,635.50

and of this total, the bonus payable to each team member (to TWO decimal places) was:

90/4 = £22.50

17 **C**

Product	Quantity	Standard time per item (hours)	Total Standard time (hours)
Buckles	50	0.2	10
Press studs	200	0.06	12
Belts	100	0.1	10
Buttons	10	0.7	7
			39

39 hours × £8 per hour = £312

18 **(a)** Complete the gaps in the table below to calculate the total labour cost for the team in May.

Labour cost	Hours	£	Working
Basic pay	500	7,500	500 × 15
Overtime rate 1	50	1,125	50 × (15 × 1.5)
Overtime rate 2	20	600	20 × (15 × 2)
Total cost before bonus	570	9,225	
Bonus		750	500 × 15 × 0.1
Total cost including bonus		9,975	

(b) **Calculate the total labour cost of painting a pole in May:**

£9,975 ÷ 3,500 = 2.85

(c) **Complete the following sentences:**

The basic pay and overtime for each member of the team in May was £9,225 ÷ 5 = £1,845

The bonus payable to each team member was £750 ÷ 5 = £150

19 (a)

Total basic pay (£)	10,800 × 9 = £97,200
Total overtime premium (£)	2,450 × 5.50 = £13,475
Hours saved (hours)	400
Bonus (£)	400 × 9 × 0.35 = £1,260
Total direct labour cost (£)	£111,935

(b)

Equivalent units	Completed	300
	CWIP 200 × 0.75	150
		——
	EU	450
Bonus (£)		0

20

Date	Code	Dr £	Cr £
6 May	5000	1,650	
6 May	4000		1,650
11 May	6000	5,750	
11 May	4000		5,750
13 May	3022	5,100	
13 May	4000		5,100
15 May (Note)	3021	5,800	
15 May	4000		5,800

Note: In practice we would need to know the reason for the overtime to decide whether to treat it as direct or indirect. This question follows the treatment in the sample assessment.

21 (a) The wages control account entries.

Wages control account

	£		£
Bank (net wages/salaries)	10,000	Maintenance (direct labour)	7,000
HMRC (income tax and NIC)	2,000	Maintenance overheads	4,000
Pension contribution	1,000	Maintenance administration	2,000
	13,000		**13,000**

(b) The total payroll cost charged to the various cost accounts of the business.

Date	Code	Debit	Credit
30 November	8200		7,000
30 November	6200	7,000	
30 November	8200		4,000
30 November	6400	4,000	
30 November	8200		2,000
30 November	6600	2,000	

22

(a) Payment of driver wages for the week amounting to 490 hours at £15.50 per hour.

	Code	£
Debit	6000	7,595
Credit	1000	7,595

(b) Drivers worked 20 hours of overtime at time and a half at the specific request of a customer. How would the overtime premium be recorded in the accounts?

	Code	£
Debit	8000	155
Credit	6000	155

(c) The stores supervisor monthly salary of £2,000.

	Code	£
Debit	9000	2,000
Credit	6000	2,000

(d) Drivers worked 10 hours of overtime at time and a half due to general work pressures. How would the overtime premium be recorded in the accounts?

	Code	£
Debit	9000	77.50
Credit	6000	77.50

JOB, BATCH AND SERVICE COSTING

23   C

	Job 812
	£
Direct materials	60
Direct labour	40
Direct expenses	20
	____
Prime cost	120
Production overheads (£40 ÷ 8) × £16	80
Non-production overheads (0.6 × £120)	72
	____
Total cost – Job 812	272

24   C

	£
Prime cost	6,840.00
Fixed overhead £300,000 ÷ 60,000 × 156	780.00
	_____
	7,620.00

Cost per unit = 7,620 ÷ 500 = **£15.24**

25   B

Average cost per occupied bed per day

$$= \frac{\text{Total cost}}{\text{Number of beds occupied}}$$

$$= \frac{£100,000 + £5,000 + £22,500}{6,450 \times 2} = £9.88$$

or £127,500/(200 × 2 + 30) × 30 = £9.88

26   C

A service is intangible and inventory cannot be held. Services generally have a high level of fixed costs and there are often difficulties in identifying a suitable cost unit.

ABSORPTION AND MARGINAL COSTING

27   B

The marginal cost of a product is the additional cost of producing an extra unit and is therefore the sum of the variable costs. If the inventory increases over a year, absorption costing profit will be higher than marginal costing profit because an element of fixed cost will be carried forward in closing inventory to be charged against profit in a future period.

28   A

Total contribution will increase as sales volume increases, but the contribution per unit will be constant as long as the sales price and variable cost per unit are unchanged. Overhead is not absorbed into the product unit so there is no under/over absorption of overhead. Marginal costing does provide useful information for decision making because it highlights contribution, which is a relevant cash flow for decision-making purposes.

29   The cost per mile under:

(a)   **Marginal costing**

Fuel and other variable overheads	£ per mile
Total variable cost per mile £9,200/4,600 miles	**2.00**

(b)   **Absorption costing**

Fuel and other variable overheads	£ per mile
Total variable cost per mile £9,200/4,600 miles	2.00
Drivers' wages, pension and national insurance £3,220/4,600 miles	0.70
Fixed overheads £23,000/4,600 miles	5.00
Total absorption cost per mile	**7.70**

30   Marginal costing

	£000	£000
Sales		50,000
Opening inventory	0	
Production costs (7,560 + 17,640)	25,200	
Closing inventory (25,200/1,800 × 800)	−11,200	
Cost of sales		−14,000
Contribution		36,000
Fixed costs (3,600 + 2,010)		−5,610
Profit for the period		30,390

Absorption costing

	£000	£000
Sales		50,000
Opening inventory	0	
Production costs (7,560 + 17,640 + 3,600)	28,800	
Closing inventory (28,800/1,800 × 800)	−12,800	
Cost of sales		−16,000
Gross Profit		34,000
Non-production cost		−2,010
Profit for the period		31,990

31 **(a)** **Marginal costing**

	£	£
Sales (12 × 12,000)		144,000
Opening inventory (7 × 2,000)	14,000	
Production costs (7 × 15,000)	105,000	
Closing inventory (7 × 5,000)	−35,000	
Cost of sales		−84,000
Contribution		60,000
Fixed costs		−30,000
Profit for the period		30,000

(b) **£36,000**

Fixed cost per unit = £30,000 ÷ 15,000 = £2 per unit

Absorption costing profit = 30,000 − FC in opening inventory + FC in closing inventory

= 30,000 − (2 × 2,000) + (2 × 5,000) = £36,000

OR

Absorption costing profit		??
Change in inventory × OAR	(2,000 − 5,000) × £2	−£6,000
Marginal costing profit		£30,000

£30,000 + £6,000 = £36,000

32 **(a)**

	£
Selling price/unit	40
Prime cost/unit	(12)
Variable production cost/unit	(4)
Contribution/unit	24

(b)

	£
Selling price/unit	40
Marginal cost/unit	(16)
Fixed production cost/unit	(10)
(£120,000/12,000 units)	
Profit/unit	14

(c) Absorption costing

	£	£
Sales (40 × 10,000)		400,000
Opening inventory (26 × 500)	13,000	
Production costs (26 × 12,000)	312,000	
Closing inventory (26 × 2,500)	−65,000	
Cost of sales		−260,000
Gross Profit		140,000
Non-production costs		0
Profit for the period		140,000

(d) **£120,000**

Total contribution = £24 × 10,000 sales units = £240,000

Profit = total contribution − total fixed costs = £240,000 − £120,000 = £120,000

OR

Absorption costing profit		£140,000
Change in inventory	(500 − 2,500) × 10 =	−20,000
Marginal costing profit		£120,000

33 B

In an absorption costing system, the fixed cost per unit would be £3,000/15,000 units = £0.20 per unit.

By switching to absorption costing, in a period when inventory levels increase by 2,000 units, absorption costing profit would be higher by 2,000 units × fixed cost per unit, i.e. by 2,000 × £0.20 = £400.

Absorption costing profit = £23,000 + £400 = £23,400.

34 (a) Calculate the estimated prime cost per batch of painted poles

£4,500 + £5,000 = £9,500

(b) Calculate the estimated marginal production cost per batch of painted poles

£9,500 + £2,500 = £12,000

(c) Calculate the estimated full absorption cost of one batch of painted poles

£12,000 + £1,750 = £13,750

ATTRIBUTING COSTS

OVERHEADS

35   D

Over-absorbed overheads increase profit, and so are recorded as a credit entry in either an over-absorbed overhead account or directly as a credit in the income statement. The matching debit entry could be either in the WIP account or the production overhead control account, depending on the costing system used.

36   C

Wages control		Overhead control	
Indirect labour × (overheads)		Indirect labour × (wages)	

OVERHEADS ALLOCATION AND APPORTIONMENT

37   D

Cost apportionment is concerned with sharing costs according to benefit received.

38   CARTCYLE LTD

	Basis of apportionment	Wood cutting £	Wood finishing £	Maintenance £	Stores £	General Admin £	Totals £
Depreciation of plant and equipment	CA of plant and equipment	1,013,229	434,241	–	–	–	1,447,470
Power for production machinery	Production machinery power usage (KwH)	772,200	514,800	–	–	–	1,287,000
Rent and rates	Floor space	–	–	94,050	56,430	37,620	188,100
Light and heat	Floor space	–	–	20,790	12,474	8,316	41,580
Indirect labour	Allocated	–	–	182,070	64,890	432,180	679,140
Totals		**1,785,429**	**949,041**	**296,910**	**133,794**	**478,116**	**3,643,290**
Reapportion Maintenance		207,837	89,073	(296,910)			
Reapportion Stores		86,966	46,828		(133,794)		
Reapportion General Admin		239,058	239,058			(478,116)	
Total overheads to production centres		2,319,290	1,324,000				3,643,290

39   AQUARIUS LTD

(a)

Overhead	Basis
Depreciation of plant and equipment	Carrying value of plant and equipment
Power for production machinery	Production machinery power usage
Rent and rates	Floor space
Light and heat	Floor space

(b)

	Basis of apportionment	Assembly £	Finishing £	Maintenance £	Stores £	Admin £	Totals £
Depreciation of plant and equipment	CA of plant and equipment	420,000	280,000	–	–	–	700,000
Power for production machinery	Production machinery power usage (KwH)	403,000	217,000	–	–	–	620,000
Rent and rates	Floor space	–	–	48,000	32,000	20,000	100,000
Light and heat	Floor space	–	–	9,600	6,400	4,000	20,000
Indirect labour	Allocated	–	–	102,000	40,000	240,000	382,000
Totals		**823,000**	**497,000**	**159,600**	**78,400**	**264,000**	**1,822,000**
Reapportion Admin		88,000	88,000	52,800	35,200	–264,000	
Reapportion Stores		56,800	34,080	22,720	–113,600		
Reapportion Maintenance		176,340	58,780	–235,120			
Total overheads to production centres		1,144,140	677,860				1,822,000

(c)   Complete the following sentences by inserting the correct values.

The fixed element of the quality control costs that will be apportioned to the Assembly department is:

£150,000 × 35% ÷ 100 × 47 = £24,675

The variable element of the quality control costs that will be apportioned to the Finishing department is:

£150,000 × 65% ÷ 100 × 62 = £60,450

40   F4L

	Basis of apportionment	Scheduled services	Charter flights	Aircraft maintenance	Fuel store	General Admin £	Totals £
		£000	£000	£000	£000	£000	£000
Depreciation of aircraft	CA of aircraft	21,840	14,560	–	–	–	36,400
Aviation fuel and other variables	Planned number of miles flown	23,210	18,990	–	–	–	42,200
Pilots and aircrew salaries	Allocated	5,250	4,709	–	–	–	9,959
Rent and rates and other premises costs	Floor space	–	–	6,300	3,780	2,520	12,600
Indirect labour	Allocated	–	–	9,600	3,200	7,800	20,600
Totals		**50,300**	**38,259**	**15,900**	**6,980**	**10,320**	**121,759**
Reapportion Maintenance and repairs		9,540	6,360	(15,900)			
Reapportion fuel and parts store		3,839	3,141		(6,980)		
Reapportion General Admin		5,160	5,160			(10,320)	
Total overheads to profit centres		68,839	52,920				121,759

41   PREMIER LABELS LTD

	Basis of apportionment	Plastics Moulding	Labelling	Stores	Equipment Maintenance	Totals
Heat and lighting fixed cost	Allocated	6,000	6,000	6,000	6,000	24,000
Heat and lighting variable cost	Square meters occupied	19,200	10,800	4,800	1,200	36,000
Power for machinery	Percentages	19,600	8,400	–	–	28,000
Supervision	Direct labour cost	50,000	70,000	–	–	120,000
Stores wages	Allocated	–	–	72,000	–	72,000
Equipment maintenance salaries	Allocated	–	–	–	188,200	188,200
Depreciation of non-current assets	CA of non-current assets	48,000	24,000	9,000	3,000	84,000
Other overhead costs	Percentages	76,800	25,600	12,800	12,800	128,000
Totals		**219,600**	**144,800**	**104,600**	**211,200**	**680,200**
Reapportion Maintenance		70,400	70,400	70,400	(211,200)	
Reapportion Stores		130,200	44,800	(175,000)		
Total overheads to profit centres		420,200	260,000			680,200

OVERHEAD ABSORPTION

42   C

An absorption rate is used to determine the full cost of a product or service. Answer A describes overhead allocation and apportionment. Absorption does not control overheads, so answer D is not correct.

43   (a)   OAR = 586,792/9,464 = £62

The correct answer is A

(b)   Absorbed = 62 × 9,745 = £604,190

The correct answer is C

(c)   Over absorption = 604,190 – 568,631 = £35,559 over absorbed

The correct answer is A

44 **(a)** Assembly = 155,000/2,000 = £77.50 and Finishing = 105,000/1,750 = £60

The correct answer is B

(b) Assembly = 155,000/12,500 = £12.40 and Finishing = 105,000/8,750 = £12

The correct answer is D

(c) Absorbed overhead = 1,750 × 90% hours × £60 = £94,500

Therefore **£24,500 under** absorbed

45 **(a)** Moulding = 36,000/18,000 = £2 and Painting = 39,000/13,000 = £3

The correct answer is D

(b) Moulding = £2 × 17,500 = £35,000 and Painting = £3 × 13,500 = £40,500

The correct answer is A

(c) Moulding = 35,000 – 37,500 = £2,500 under absorbed and Painting = 40,500 – 40,000 = 500 over absorbed.

The correct answer is B

46 **(a)** Mixing = 64,800/10,000 = £6.48 and Bagging = 70,200/2,340 = £30.00

The correct answer is A

(b) Mixing = £6.48 × 9,000 = £58,320 and Bagging = £30.00 × 2,120 = £63,600

The correct answer is C

(c) Mixing = 58,320 – 67,500 = £9,180 under absorbed and Bagging = 63,600 – 75,600 = £12,000 under absorbed.

The correct answer is B

(d) Complete the following sentence

An under absorption of overheads will be **debited** to the Profit and Loss account. This will **increase** expenses and will **decrease** profit.

47 **A**

Under or over-absorption is determined by comparing the actual overhead expenditure with the overhead absorbed.

48 **D**

Fixed production overheads are over-absorbed when actual expenditure is less than budget and/or actual production volume is higher than budget.

ACTIVITY BASED COSTING

49 D

Statement (1) provides a definition of a cost driver. Cost drivers for long-term variable overhead costs will be the volume of a particular activity to which the cost driver relates, so Statement (2) is correct. Statement (3) is also correct. In traditional absorption costing, standard high-volume products receive a higher amount of overhead costs than with ABC. ABC allows for the unusually high costs of support activities for low-volume products (such as relatively higher set-up costs, order processing costs and so on).

50 A

51 (a) C

$$\text{Overhead absorption rate} = \frac{\text{Total overhead cost}}{\text{Total number of direct labour hours}}$$

Total overhead cost = 90,000 + 150,000 + 180,000 = £420,000

Total direct labour hours = (5 × 1,200) + (5 × 10,800) = 60,000 direct labour hours

Overhead absorption rate = £420,000 ÷ 60,000 direct labour hours

Overhead absorption rate = £7.00 per labour hour.

Alpha uses 5 direct labour hours per unit so will have an overhead cost per unit of 5 hours × £7.00 per hour = £35.00

(b) C

The overhead cost per unit for each unit of product Beta will be the same as product Alpha, as both products use the same number of labour hours (5 hours).

(c) D

	Labour related	Purchasing related	Set-up related
Costs	£90,000	£150,000	£180,000
Consumption of activities (cost drivers)	60,000 labour hours	150 purchase orders	100 set-ups
Cost per unit of cost driver	£1.50 per labour hour	£1,000 per purchase order	£1,800 per set-up
Costs per product			
Product Alpha:	£1.50 × 6,000 labour hours = £9,000	£1,000 × 70 purchase orders = £70,000	£1,800 × 40 set-ups = £72,000
Product Beta:	£1.50 × 54,000 labour hours = £81,000	£1,000 × 80 purchase orders = £80,000	£1,800 × 60 set-ups = £108,000

Total overhead cost for Alpha = £9,000 + £70,000 + £72,000 = £151,000. Spread over 1,200 units, this represents a cost per unit of £125.83

(d) B

Total overhead cost for Beta = £81,000 + £80,000 + £108,000 = £269,000. Spread over 10,800 units, this represents a cost per unit of £24.91

52   C

Cost pool = £84,000

Cost driver = number of set-ups

Set ups A = 40,000 ÷ 2,000 = 20

Set ups B = 40,000 ÷ 5,000 = 8

Total set-ups 20 + 8 = 28

Rate per set up =£84,000 ÷ 28 = £3,000 per set-up

Cost for B = £3,000 × 8 set-ups = £24,000

Per unit = £24,000/40,000 = £0.60.

53   DOG

Workings:

Machine department

Total cost £20,800

Total machine hours = (8 × 240) + (6 × 200) + (4 × 160) + (6 × 240) = 5,200 hours

Cost per hour = £20,800 ÷ 5,200 hours = £4.00 per hour

W = £4 × 8hr × 240 units = £7,680

X = £4 × 6hr × 200 units = £4,800

Y = £4 × 4hr × 160 units = £2,560

Z = £4 × 6hr × 240 units = £5,760

Set up

Total cost £10,500

Total production runs = (240 + 200 + 160 + 240) ÷ 40 = 21 runs

Cost per run = £10,500 ÷ 21 = £500 per run

W = £500 × (240 ÷ 40) = £3,000

X = £500 × (200 ÷ 40) = £2,500

Y = £500 × (160 ÷ 40) = £2,000

Z = £500 × (240 ÷ 40) = £3,000

Stores receiving

Total cost £7,200

Total requisitions raised = 40 × 4 = 160

Cost per requisition = £7,200 ÷ 160 = £45 per requisition

W = £45 × 40 = £1,800

X = £45 × 40 = £1,800

Y = £45 × 40 = £1,800

Z = £45 × 40 = £1,800

Total costs	W	X	Y	Z
	£	£	£	£
Direct materials	19,200	20,000	9,600	28,800
Direct labour	13,440	8,400	4,480	10,080
Machine department costs	7,680	4,800	2,560	5,760
Set up costs	3,000	2,500	2,000	3,000
Stores receiving	1,800	1,800	1,800	1,800
Total cost	45,120	37,500	20,440	49,440
Cost per unit	188.00	187.50	127.75	206.00

SHORT TERM DECISION MAKING

COST BEHAVIOURS

54   C

	£
Total cost of 18,500 hours	251,750
Total cost of 17,000 hours	246,500
Variable cost of 1,500 hours	5,250

Variable cost per machine hour = £5,250/1,500 machine hours = £3.50.

	£
Total cost of 17,000 hours	246,500
Less variable cost of 17,000 hours (× £3.50)	59,500
Balance = fixed costs	187,000

55   A

	Cost per unit (£) (125 units)	Cost per unit (£) (180 units)
T1	8.00	7.00
T2	14.00	14.00
T3	19.80	15.70
T4	25.80	25.80

Cost types T2 and T4 are variable and T1 and T3 are semi-variable.

56

	Description
Variable cost	Increase in total as volume increases
Fixed cost	Decreases per unit as volume increases
Stepped cost	Fixed for a certain volume range only
Semi-variable cost	Made up of fixed and variable costs

57 Graph 1 C; Graph 2 D

58 TRUCK TRANSPORT

Cost	Classification (tick correct answer)				Total cost at 5,000 miles (£)
	Variable	Semi-variable	Fixed	Stepped fixed	
Cost 1				✓	27,000
Cost 2	✓				35,000
Cost 3			✓		31,500
Cost 4		✓			39,000

Working for Cost 4

Total cost at lowest level = 1,500 × £12.00 = £18,000

Total cost at highest level = 6,000 × £7.50 = £45,000

VC per unit = (£45,000 – £18,000)/(6,000 – 1,500) = £6.00

Total fixed cost = £45,000 – (6,000 × £6.00) = £9,000

Total cost at 5,000 units = £9,000 + (5,000 × £6.00) = £39,000

59   CARTCYCLE LTD

Batches produced and sold	2,160	2,700	3,600
	£	£	£
Sales revenue	64,800	81,000	108,000
Variable costs:			
• Direct materials	9,720	12,150	16,200
• Direct labour	22,680	28,350	37,800
• Overheads	12,960	16,200	21,600
Semi-variable costs:	6,804		
• Variable element		5,400	7,200
• Fixed element		2,484	2,484
Total cost	52,164	64,584	85,284
Total profit	12,636	16,416	22,716
Profit per batch (to 2 decimal places)	5.85	6.08	6.31

60   CHARTER FLIGHTS

Likely miles	5,000	6,000	7,000
	£000	£000	£000
Sale revenue	2,500	2,950	3,400
Variable/semi-variable costs:			
• Aviation fuel	400	480	560
• Landing and servicing fees	850	900	950
• Other variable overheads	135	162	189
Fixed costs:			
• Wages and salaries	420	420	420
• Other fixed overheads	625	625	625
Total cost	2430	2,587	2,744
Total profit	70	363	656
Profit per mile flown (2 d.p.) £	14.00	60.50	93.71

61 **(a)** **£24,000 ÷ 800 = £30**

(b) VC = £3,600 + £8,400 + £1,800 = £13,800

VC per unit = £13,800 ÷ 800 = £17.25

SV VC per unit = (£4,920 – £2,520) ÷ (1,600 – 800) = £3.00

Total VC per unit = **£20.25**

(c) FC = £2,520 – (800 × 3) = £120

FC per unit = £120 ÷ 1,200 = **£0.10**

(d) Total cost = (£20.25 × 1,500) + 120 = £30,495

Total cost per unit = £30,495 ÷ 1,500 = **£20.33**

(e) Contribution per unit = £30 – £20.25 = £9.75

Total contribution = £9.75 × 1,500 = £14,625

Total profit = £14,625 – £120 = £14,505

Profit per unit = £14,505 ÷ 1,500 = **£9.67**

SEGMENTAL REPORTING

62 **(a)**

	Route S	Route SE	Route SW
Contract miles	3,000	3,000 × 80% = 2,400	3,000 × 1.20 = 3,600
Revenue and costs			
Revenue (£000s)	3,000 × £150 = £450,000 **450**	2,400 × £150 × 1.1 = 396,000 **396**	3,600 × £150 × 90% = 486,000 **486**
Variable costs (£000s)	3,000 × £80 £240,000 **240**	2,400 × £85 = £204,000 **204**	3,600 × £80 × 93.75% = £270,000 **270**
Contribution (£000)	450 – 240 = **210**	396 – 204 = **192**	486 – 270 = **216**
Fixed costs (£000)	80	120	200
Profit (£000s)	130	72	16

63 INDIA LTD

	Rose (£)	Tulip (£)	Buttercup (£)	Total (£)
Selling price per unit	50.00	120.00	80.00	
Less: Variable costs per units				
Direct material	10.00	24.00	16.00	
Direct labour	13.00	44.00	21.00	
Contribution per unit	27.00	52.00	43.00	
Sales volume (units)	1,000	200	500	
Total contribution	27,000	10,400	21,500	58,900
Less: fixed costs				52,000
Budgeted profit				6,900

64 SPORT SHIRT LTD

(a)

	New £	Existing £	Total £
Sales revenue	24,000	60,000	
Less: variable costs			
Direct materials	7,500	12,000	
Direct labour	2,500	7,500	
Total contribution	14,000	40,500	54,500
Less: fixed costs			33,750
Budgeted profit			20,750

COST VOLUME PROFIT ANALYSIS

65 Choose the correct description for each of the following:

Term
Contribution
Breakeven point
Margin of safety

Description
Selling price less variable costs
Sales units where is no profit or loss
Excess of actual sales over breakeven sales

66 (a) **£7.20 × 9,000 = £64,800**

(b) $\dfrac{64,800}{41.40 - 27} = 4,500$ units

(c)

Units of MR 13 sold	9,000
Margin of safety (units)	9,000 – 4,500 = 4,500 units
Margin of safety percentage	$\dfrac{9,000 - 4,500}{9,000} \times 100 = 50\%$

(d) The correct answer is **A** – an increase in selling price means that contribution per unit increases therefore fewer units have to be made to cover the fixed costs. If BEP is lower than the margin of safety is higher.

(e)

	Product MR13
Number of units to be sold to meet target profit	$\dfrac{£36,000 + £64,800}{£14.40} = 7,000$ units
Revised margin of safety (%)	$\dfrac{9,000 - 7,000}{9,000} \times 100 = 22.22\%$
Revised margin of safety in sales revenue (£)	$2,000 \times £41.40 = £82,800$

67 **(a)** Contribution = £0.80 – £0.30 = £0.50

£312,500 ÷ £0.50 × £0.80 = £500,000

OR using the PV ratio $\dfrac{£312,500}{£0.50/£0.80} = £500,000$

(b) Using the PV ratio = $\dfrac{£312,500 + £200,000}{£0.50/£0.80} = £820,000$

(c) (i) £875,000 – £500,000 = £375,000

(ii) £375,000/£500,000 × 100 = 75%

68 **(a)**

	A (£)	B (£)	Total (£)
Selling price per unit	1.50	1.20	
Less: variable costs per unit			
Direct materials	0.20	0.25	
Direct labour	0.12	0.14	
Variable overheads	0.15	0.19	
Contribution per unit	1.03	0.62	
Sales volume (units)	300,000	500,000	
Total contribution	309,000	310,000	619,000
Less: fixed costs			264,020
Budgeted profit or loss			354,980

(b)

Product	A	B
Fixed costs (£)	158,620	105,400
Unit contribution (£)	1.03	0.62
Break-even sales (units)	154,000	170,000
Forecast sales (units)	250,000	400,000
Margin of safety (units)	96,000	230,000
Margin of safety (%)	38.40	57.50

(c)

Product A		Product B	✓

69 **(a)**

Likely miles	10,000	12,000	14,000
	£	£	£
Sales revenue	100,000	120,000	140,000
Variable costs:			
• Fuel	8,000	9,600	11,200
• Drivers' wages and associated costs	5,000	6,000	7,000
• Overheads	6,000	7,200	8,400
Fixed costs:			
• Indirect labour	10,600	10,600	10,600
• Overheads	25,850	25,850	25,850
Total cost	55,450	59,250	63,050
Total profit	44,550	60,750	76,950
Profit per mile	4.455	5.063	5.496

(b)

Forecast number of miles		12,000	14,000
Sales revenue	£	120,000	140,000
Fixed costs	£	36,450	
Contribution	£	97,200	
Contribution per mile	£	8.10	
Break-even number of miles	Miles	4,500	
Break-even sales revenue	£	45,000	
Margin of safety in number of miles	Miles	7,500	9,500
Margin of safety in sales revenue	£	75,000	95,000
Margin of safety	%	62.50	67.86

70   Line A is total revenue

Line B is total costs

Line C is total variable costs

Line D is fixed costs

71   (a)   **Calculate the breakeven volume of 0.8m poles:**

Contribution per unit = 10 − [(75 + 200 + 250) ÷ 150] = £6.50

BEP = £325 ÷ £6.50 = 50 units

(b)   **Calculate the breakeven sales revenue of 0.8m poles.**

50 units × £10 = £500

(c)   **How many 2.8m poles must Jump sell to reach its target profit of £2,400.**

Target profit = (£450 + £2,400) ÷ (£1,500 ÷ 50) = 95 poles

(d)   **Calculate the margin of safety of the 2.8m pole (in poles).**

Contribution per pole = (£1,500 ÷ 50) = £30

BEP = £450 ÷ £30 = 15 poles

Target sales = (£450 + £2,400) ÷ £30 = 95 poles

Margin of safety = 95 − 15 = 80 poles

PRINCIPLES OF BUDGETING AND CASH MANAGEMENT

BUDGETING

72

to give authority to spend	✓
to control expenditure	✓
to aid decision making.	

The main purposes of budgeting are to plan and control. Budgets also usually give authority to spend up to the budget limit. Budgets are not primarily used for decision making.

73   C

74

	Characteristic of rolling budgets?
Budgets are more likely to be realistic as there is a shorter period between preparation and actual events occurring	
Updates to budgets are only made when they are foreseeable	✓
They reduce uncertainty in budgeting	
They force management to look ahead more frequently	
Each item of expenditure must be fully justified before inclusion in the budget	✓

Rolling budgets are updated on as regular basis (for example, monthly or quarterly), not just when a change is foreseeable. The final point is a characteristic of zero based budgeting.

75   B

Option C is a fixed budget and option D is a rolling budget. Option A is incorrect as a flexible budget includes all costs.

76

A fixed budget is a budget that considers all of an organisation's costs and revenues for a single level of activity.	✓
A flexible budget is a budget that is produced during the budget period to recognise the effects of any changes in prices and methods of operation that have occurred.	
Organisations can use budgets to communicate objectives to their managers.	✓

A fixed budget is prepared for a single level of activity. A flexible budget is prepared during the budget period but it recognises only the effects of changes in the volume of activity. A major purpose of the budgetary planning exercise is to communicate an organisation's objectives to its managers.

77

	Workings:	£
Raw material	5 kg × £7.50 per kg	37.50
Labour	2 hours × £7.50 per hour	15.00
Variable overhead	2 hours × £2 per hour	4.00
Fixed overhead	2 hours × £5 per hour	10.00
Standard cost for one unit		66.50

CASH MANAGEMENT

78   D

Options A and B would affect both cash flow and profits. Option C would affect the profits but not the cash flow. Option D is a receipt that would increase cash flow but would not affect profits.

79

Item	Cash	Profit	Cash and profit
Depreciation on a machine		X	
Selling a non-current asset for its carry value	X		
Repaying a bank loan	X		
Prepaying next year's rent	X		
Making a cash sale			X

80   C

81   D

82

(a)   **A**

(300/2,700) × 365 = 40.55 days

(b)   **B**

(230/1,300) × 365 = 64.58 days

(c)   **D**

(150/1,300) × 365 = 42.12 days

(d)   **A**

41 + 42 − 65 = 18 days

83   The working capital cycle for the business is **48 days.**

	Days
Raw materials inventory holding period	8
Less: trade payables payment period	(28)
WIP holding period	4
Finished goods holding period	26
Trade receivables' collection period	38
	———
Working capital cycle (days)	48
	———

Note: add the assets and subtract the liabilities

84 **(a)**

	Working	30 June 20X2
Sales revenue	Receivable days = Rec ÷ Rev × 365 22 = 145,000 ÷ Rev × 365 Rev = 145,000 ÷ 22 × 365	2,405,682
Cost of sales	2,405,685 − 500,000	1,905,682
Inventories level in the statement of financial position	Inventory days = Inv ÷ COS × 365 47 = Inv ÷ 1,905,682 × 365 Inv = 47 ÷ 365 × 1,905,682	245,389
Trade payables payment period in days (1 decimal place)	95,000 ÷ 1,905,682 × 365	18

(b) The cash operating cycle for GH is 22 + 47 − 18 = 51 days

85

(a) **March**

(b) **April**

86

Action	Positive	Negative
Delay paying suppliers	✓	
Extend the credit terms currently offered to customers		✓
Offer credit to new customers		✓
Reduce the credit terms currently offered to customers	✓	
Extending credit terms with suppliers	✓	
Paying suppliers on receipt of an invoice		✓
Increasing credit limits to existing customers		✓

PREPARATION OF BUDGETS

PREPARATION OF BUDGETS

87

		£
Skilled		
Product A	875 units × 1.5 hours/unit × £12/hour	15,750
Product B	2,500 units × 1 hours/unit × £12/hour	30,000
Unskilled		
Product A	875 units × 2.5 hours/unit × £8/hour	17,500
Product B	2,500 units × 2 hours/unit × £8/hour	40,000
		————
		103,250
		————

88   D

Paid hours including idle time = 1,350 × 100/90 = 1,500

Budgeted labour cost = 1,500 hours × £ = £10,500

89   B

	£
Purchases on credit	180,000
Increase in trade payables	−7,500
	————
Therefore payments to suppliers	172,500
	————

An increase in trade payables means that the company is buying more on credit that they are paying back to their suppliers, for example:

Trade payables

	£		£
Cash paid	**172,500**	Opening balance	3,000
Closing balance 3,000 + 7,500	10,500	Purchases	180,000
	————		————
	183,000		183,000
	————		————

90   £252,000

	£
Budgeted sales	120,000
Expected decrease in receivables	+ 6,000
	————
	126,000
	————

A reduction in receivables means that the company will expect to receive more cash next month than the total of its credit sales for the month, for example:

Trade receivables

	£		£
Opening balance	10,000	Cash received	**126,000**
Sales	120,000	Closing balance 10,000 – 6,000	4,000
	———		———
	130,000		130,000

91   B

	£
July's sales £12,500 × 20%	2,500
June's sales £10,000 × 60%	6,000
May's sales £15,000 × 10%	1,500
	———
	10,000
	———

92   £2,271

	April £
January 30 % × 2,570	771
February 50% × 2,000	1,000
March 20% × 2,500	500
Total	2,271

93

Depreciation	✓
Provisions for doubtful debts	✓
Wages and salaries	

Depreciation and the provision for doubtful debts are not cash flow items and so would not be included in a cash budget.

BUDGETS AND DEVIATIONS

VARIANCE ANALYSIS

94

An adverse variance increases profit	
A favourable variance increases profit	✓
A favourable variance will arise when actual revenue is greater than budgeted revenue	✓
An adverse variance will arise when actual costs are greater than budgeted costs	✓

95 **(a)** **£450 favourable.**

Variable overhead flexed budget = £5,000 ÷ 10,000 × 9,500 = £4,750.

Variance = £4,750 − £4,300 = £450 favourable

(b) **£200 adverse**.

Variance = £5,000 − £5,200 = £200 adverse.

96 **AQUARIUS LTD**

	Flexed budget	Actual	Variance	Favourable F or Adverse A
Volume sold	267,000	267,000		
	£000	£000	£000	
Sales revenue	2,136	2,409	273	F
Less costs:				
Direct materials	534	801	267	A
Direct labour	267	267	0	0
Fixed overheads	600	750	150	A
Profit from operations	735	591	144	A

97   GRAPE LTD

(a)

	Original budget	Flexed budget	Actual	Variance
Volume sold	20,000	28,800	28,800	
	£000	£000	£000	£000
Sales revenue	3,000	4,320	3,877	−443
Less costs:				
Direct materials	175	252	212	40
Direct labour	875	1,260	912	348
Variable overheads	445	641	448	193
Fixed overheads	300	300	325	−25
Profit from operations	1,205	1,867	1,980	113

(b)   C

(c)   C

98   GLOBE LTD

(a)

	Original budget	Flexed budget	Actual	Variance
Volume sold	4,000	5,000	5,000	
	£000	£000	£000	£000
Sales revenue	1,500	1,875	1,950	75
Less costs:				
Direct materials	36	45	45	0
Direct labour	176	220	182	38
Variable overheads	92	115	90	25
Profit from operations	1,196	1,495	1,633	138

(b)   B

(c)   D

The flexed budget has already taken account of the increase in units sold, offering a bulk discount should increase units sales but at a reduced price, increased competition from other companies could lead to a reduction in sales units and prices.

SPREADSHEETS FOR MANAGEMENT ACCOUNTS

99   C

By definition.

100   B

A spreadsheet programme can convert numerical data into the form of a graph, pie chart or bar chart, as required, but it cannot produce a narrative description.

101   C

A database contains records and files and is most suitable for storing large volumes of data

102   A

All are said to be advantages of spreadsheet automatic calculation helps with speed and accuracy, the ability to display data in different ways help with legibility and variety.

103   C

The correct syntax has an = sign and a colon.

104   D

The number will appear with a percentage sign after it. Most Excel spreadsheets will work to two decimal places by default.

105   A

Rounding 10.567 will give 11.

106   B

The symbol $ makes a cell address absolute.

107   A

Total commission = total sales × 5% = (home sales + overseas sales) × 5%

108   D

The standard 40 hour week needs to be 'held' to compare with the employees actual hours in cells C10 to C14. Using the $ sign next to B and 2 will do this.

109   A

To SORT the price column C, you would need to select the data range A2:C5, right click, data, sort, choose to sort column C.

110 A

Number is the number or cell reference to round, *digits* is the number of digits to round the number to. To illustrate this: if the digit is set to 1 it will round to 1 decimal place, 2 will round to 2 decimal places. Alternatively, if the digit is set to -1 it will round to the nearest 10, -2 will round to the nearest 100.

111 D

The excel answers to the scenario questions can be within the MATS course on MyKaplan.

Please go to www.mykaplan.co.uk and login using your username and password.

Section 3

MOCK ASSESSMENT QUESTIONS

TASK 1 (24 MARKS)

This task is about costing techniques

Sarloue has the following information available for superfine oil S07:

Date purchased	Quantity (litres)	Cost per litre (£)	Total cost (£)
5 July	625	2.20	1,375
16 July	550	2.40	1,320
22 July	650	2.50	1,625

(a) **Calculate the cost of an issue of 600 litres on 20 July and the inventory balance at the end of the month (round to the nearest £).** **(4 marks)**

	Cost (£)
AVCO issue	
AVCO balance	
FIFO issue	
FIFO balance	

Below is a weekly timesheet for one of Sarloue's employees, who is paid as follows:

- For a basic seven and a half hour shift every day from Monday to Friday – basic pay.

- For any overtime in excess of the basic seven and a half hours, on any day from Monday to Friday – the extra hours are paid at time-and-a-half.

(b) Complete the columns headed Basic pay, overtime premium and Total pay. (**Note** Zero figures should be entered in cells where appropriate). **(6 marks)**

Employee's weekly timesheet for week ending 21 July

Employee:		A. Lander	Profit centre:			Warehouse	
Employee number:		S007	Basic pay per hour:			£8.00	
	Total hours spent in work	Hours spent on indirect work	Notes	Basic pay £	Overtime premium £	Total pay £
Monday	8	½	Overtime is a customer request			
Tuesday	7½					
Wednesday	8	½	Early delivery			
Thursday	8	½	Overtime is a customer request			
Friday	7½					
Total	**39**	**1½**				

(c) Which of the following double entry journal(s) would be required to correctly account for the overtime premium? **(2 marks)**

	Tick
Dr Production £4, Cr Wages £4	
Dr Overheads £4, Cr Wages £4	
Dr Production £2, Cr Wages £2	
Dr Overheads £2, Cr Wages £2	
Dr Production £6, Cr Wages £6	
Dr Overheads £6, Cr Wages £6	

Sarloue uses both batch and unit costing, as appropriate, in its plastic extrusion department. It is currently costing a new product LL45. LL45 will be produced in batches of 4,500.

It has been estimated that the following costs will be incurred in producing one batch of 4,500 units of LL45.

Product LL45	£
Direct materials £ per unit	6.00
Direct labour £ per unit	5.50
Variable overheads £ per batch	14,625
Total fixed manufacturing overheads	36,000
Total fixed administration, selling and distribution costs	19,170

(d) **Calculate the estimated prime cost of per unit of LL45:** **(2 marks)**

£

(e) **Calculate the estimated marginal production cost of one batch of LL45:** **(2 marks)**

£

(f) **Calculate the estimated total full absorption cost of one batch of LL45:** **(2 marks)**

£

(g) **Calculate the estimated marginal cost per unit of LL45:** **(2 marks)**

£

(h) **Calculate the estimated full absorption cost per unit of LL45:** **(2 marks)**

£

(i) **A cost centre is defined as:** **(2 marks)**

A   A unit of product or service for which costs are accumulated

B   A production or service location, function, activity or item of equipment for which costs are accumulated

C   Costs that relate directly to a unit

D   Costs that contain both a fixed and a variable element

TASK 2 (24 MARKS)

This task is about attributing costs

(a)   Why might Sarloue decide to allocate its costs between the products of different departments? (2 marks)

   A   To reduce its overall inventory valuation

   B   To comply with accounting standards

   C   To report segmented profits/losses

   D   To speed up its internal reporting

Sarloue's budgeted overheads for the next financial year are:

	£	£
Depreciation of plant and equipment		135,000
Power for production machinery		17,500
Rent and rates		23,750
Light and heat		6,250
Indirect labour costs:		
Maintenance	10,000	
Stores	12,500	
Canteen	36,000	
Total indirect labour cost		58,500

The following information is also available:

Department	Carrying amount of plant and equipment	Production machinery power usage (KwH)	Floor space (square metres)	Number of employees
Production centres:				
Plastic moulding	180,000	22,500	2,000	20
Plastic extrusion	360,000	30,000	2,000	20
Support cost centres:				
Maintenance			1,000	2
Stores			3,000	2
Canteen			2,000	2
Total	540,000	52,500	10,000	46

Overheads are allocated or apportioned on the most appropriate basis. The total overheads of the support cost centres are then reapportioned on the follow bases:

- 60% of the Maintenance cost centre's time is spent maintaining production machinery in the Plastic moulding production centre and 30% of time is spent in the Plastic extrusion production centre. The remainder is spent maintaining the canteen equipment

- The Stores cost centre supports the two production centres equally

- The Canteen cost centre is reapportioned based on staff numbers in the two production centres only.

(b) **Complete the overhead analysis table below:** **(14 marks)**

	Basis	Plastic moulding £	Plastic extrusion £	Maintenance £	Stores £	Canteen £	Totals £
Depreciation of plant and equipment							
Power for production machinery	KwH hours	7,500	10,000	0	0	0	17,500
Rent and rates	Floor space	4,750	4,750	2,375	7,125	4,750	23,750
Light and heat							
Indirect labour	Allocated	1,250	1,250	625	1,875	1,250	6,250
Totals		**58,500**	**106,000**	**13,000**	**21,500**	**42,000**	**241,000**
Reapportion Maintenance							
Reapportion Stores							
Reapportion Canteen							
Total overheads to production centres							241,000

Sarloue's budgeted overheads and activity levels are:

	Plastic moulding	Plastic extrusion
Budgeted overheads (£)	22,500	24,750
Budgeted direct labour hours	5,000	5,200
Budgeted machine hours	15,000	20,000

(c)   What would the budgeted overhead absorption rate for each department, if this were set based on being labour intensive, to the nearest penny?   **(2 marks)**

	Plastic moulding £	Plastic extrusion £
Budgeted overhead absorption rate	per hour	per hour

Additional data

At the end of the quarter actual overheads incurred were found to be:

	Plastic moulding £	Plastic extrusion £
Actual overheads	19,800	28,000

Overheads were recovered on a labour hour basis. The labour hours were 5% more than budgeted in Plastic moulding and 3% more in Plastic extrusion.

(d)   Calculate the overhead that was absorbed in each department and state the under or over absorption that occurred in each department (answers to the nearest £).   **(4 marks)**

	Actual hours worked	Absorbed amount £	Under/over	Value £
Plastic moulding				
Plastic extrusion				

Additional data

The overhead absorption rate in the plastic moulding department should have been based on machine hours. The actual machine hours for the period were 14,500 hours.

(e)   Complete the following table: **(2 marks)**

	Overhead absorption rate £	Overhead absorbed £	Under/over absorption £
Plastics moulding department	per hour		Under/over

TASK 3 (24 MARKS)

This task is about short term decision making

Sarloue has a new trainee management accountant and your manager would like you to help with training.

(a)   Match the following descriptions to the type of cost behaviour   **(4 marks)**

Behaviour		Description
Variable cost		Decreases per unit as volume increases
Fixed cost		Fixed for a certain volume range only
Stepped cost		Made up of fixed and variable costs
Semi-variable cost		Increase in total as volume increases

Sarloue wishes to make a profit of £11,500 and has a contract with a customer to produce 5,000 litres of GG99. Revenues and costs for 5,000 litres are shown below.

Possible production level	5,000 litres
	£
Sales revenue	145,000
Variable and semi-variable costs:	
Material	30,000
Labour	40,000
Overheads	25,000
Fixed costs:	
Indirect labour	20,000
Overheads	15,000
Target profit for contract	11,500

The labour cost is a semi-variable cost. The fixed cost is £20,000 and the variable cost is £4.00 per unit.

(b) **Use the table below to calculate whether this contract will achieve its target profit. Enter the contribution per litre to two decimal places.** **(16 marks)**

Calculation of required number of litres	£
Fixed costs	
Target profit	
Fixed cost and target profit	
Sales revenue	
Variable costs	
Contribution	
Contribution per unit	
Required number of litres to achieve target profit	

(c) **Based on your answers in (b), what is the breakeven point** (round down to the nearest litre)? **(2 marks)**

units

(d) **Based on your answers above, what is the margin of safety?** **(2 marks)**

%

TASK 4 (16 MARKS)

This task is about understanding principles of budgeting and of cash management

(a)   **Why is liquidity management important?** (2 marks)

    A   Liquidity management is important to ensure that a company does not make a loss.

    B   Liquidity management is important so that the shareholders can see how much return they will get on their investment.

    C   Liquidity management is important so that the company can estimate how much cash is tied up in inventory and non-current assets.

    D   Liquidity management is important so that the company can ensure that cash is available to discharge commitments.

Sarloue expects to use 2,000 labour hours to manufacture 500 units of one of its components in a month.

(b)   **The standard labour time in hours required for a unit is:** (2 marks)

hours

(c)   **Which TWO of the following are benefits of budgeting?** (2 marks)

It helps coordinate the activities of different departments	
It establishes a system of control	
It fulfils legal reporting obligations	
It is a starting point for strategic planning	

(d)   **Which of the following statement(s) is/are true regarding different types of budget?**

(2 marks)

	True	False
A flexible budget can be used to control operational efficiency		
Rolling budgets review and, if necessary, revise the budget for the next period to ensure that budgets remain relevant for the remainder of the accounting period		

(e)   **Which TWO of the following statements about budgets and standards are true?** (2 marks)

	Tick
Budgets can be used in situations where output cannot be measured, but standards cannot be used in such situations	
Budgets are used for planning purposes, standards are used only for control purposes	
Budgets can include allowances for inefficiencies in operations, but standards use performance targets which are attainable under the most favourable conditions	
Standards which remain unaltered for long periods of time are referred to as basic standards	

Sarloue has gathered the following information for the year ended 31 December 20X4

Sales revenue	£2,600,000
Cost of sales	£1,800,000
Purchases (of which 90% were on credit)	£1,650,000
Trade payables	£260,000
Trade receivables collection period	58 days
Inventory	£220,000

(f) **Calculate the following to the nearest whole day.** **(4 marks)**

	days
Trade payables payment period	
Inventory holding period	

(g) **The cash operating cycle for Sarloue is:** **(2 marks)**

	days

TASK 5 (16 MARKS)

This task is about the preparation of budgets.

Open the 'Kit Mock Task 5 data' worksheet from MyKaplan.

Sarloue Ltd has prepared a forecast for the next quarter for three of its engineered components, GG57, HH23 and KK12.

The company expects to produce and sell 1,000 GG57 and 1,500 HH23. The budgeted sales demand for KK12 is 25% greater than that of HH23. Budgeted total fixed costs are £12,750.

On the 'Budget' worksheet

(a) Copy and paste the sales volumes for GG57 and HH23 from the 'Data' worksheet to cells B2 and C2 **(1 mark)**

(b) Use a formula to calculate the sales volume for KK12 in cell D2 **(1 mark)**

(c) In row 4 calculate the sales revenue per unit for each component, rounding the value to two decimal places **(2 marks)**

(d) In rows 6 to 8 calculate the variable costs per unit for each component. Use absolute referencing, where appropriate, and round each value to two decimal places **(2 marks)**

(e) In row 9 calculate the contribution per unit for each component **(1 mark)**

(f) In row 10 calculate the total contribution earned for each component **(1 mark)**

(g) Complete the total column for rows 2 and 10 **(1 mark)**

The fixed costs are to be apportioned based on sales volume (units).

(h) Copy and paste the total fixed costs from the 'Data' worksheet into cell E11. Calculate the apportioned fixed costs in cells B11 to D11 and round to the nearest £ **(2 marks)**

(i) Calculate the budgeted profit or loss in cell E12 **(1 mark)**

(j) In cell F12 use an IF statement to show if the budget produces a 'profit' or a 'loss' **(2 marks)**

(k) In cell A14 add the title 'Breakeven point'. In cells B14:D14 calculate the breakeven point for each component. Round appropriately. **(2 marks)**

TASK 6 **(16 MARKS)**

This task is about budgets and deviations

Open the 'Kit Mock Task 6 data' worksheet from MyKaplan.

Sarloue Ltd has the following original budget and actual performance for product GG101 for the year ending 31 December.

On the 'Variances' worksheet

(a) In cell J1 calculate the percentage change required to flex the budgeted activity to match the actual activity. Format the cell to percentage, two decimal places **(2 marks)**

(b) Calculate the flexed the budget in cell C4 and C6:C8 by referencing the contents of cell J1 using absolute referencing were appropriate and using appropriate formula **(2 marks)**

(c) Calculate the flexed profit in cell C9, format the values with thousands separator and no decimal places, using appropriate formula **(2 mark)**

(d) In cells E4 and E6:E9 calculate the variances in £ using appropriate formula, indicate an adverse variance with a minus sign. **(2 mark)**

(e) In cells F4 and F6:F9 calculate the variance percentage of budget using appropriate formula, format the values to the nearest whole percent. **(2 mark)**

Your manager would like to be informed of any significant variances. A significant variance is one that is more than 10% of budget.

(f) Use conditional formatting to highlight any significant variances for your manager. The cells should be filled in red. **(2 marks)**

(g) In cells G4 and G5:G9 use an IF and AND statement to say 'investigate' if the variance is significant, the cell should stay blank if investigation is not required **(2 marks)**

Your manager would like to see how the total cost is split over the different costs in the budget

(g) Produce a pie chart on the 'Variances' worksheet to show the actual costs as a proportion of the whole cost. Give the pie chart a suitable title, a legend on the right and add data labels as percentages to each segment. **(2 marks)**

Section 4

ANSWERS TO MOCK ASSESSMENT QUESTIONS

TASK 1

(a)

	Cost (£)
AVCO issue	1,376
AVCO balance	2,944
FIFO issue	1,320
FIFO balance	3,000

(b)

Employee's weekly timesheet for week ending 21 July

Employee:	A. Lander		Profit centre:			Warehouse store man
Employee number:	S007		**Basic pay per hour:**	£8.00		
	Total hours spent in work	Hours spent on indirect work	Notes	Basic pay £	Overtime premium £	Total pay £
Monday	8	½	Overtime is a customer request	64	2	66
Tuesday	7½			60	0	60
Wednesday	8	½	Early delivery	64	2	66
Thursday	8	½	Overtime is a customer request	64	2	66
Friday	7½			60	0	60
Total	**39**	**1½**		312	6	318

(c)

	Tick
Dr Production £4, Cr Wages £4	✓
Dr Overheads £4, Cr Wages £4	
Dr Production £2, Cr Wages £2	✓
Dr Overheads £2, Cr Wages £2	
Dr Production £6, Cr Wages £6	
Dr Overheads £6, Cr Wages £6	

(d)   £6.00 + £5.50 = £11.50

(e)   (£11.50 × 4,500) + £14,625 = £66,375

(f)   £66,375 + £36,000 = £102,375

(g)   £66,375 ÷ 4,500 = £14.75

(h)   £102,375 ÷ 4,500 = £22.75

(i)   B

TASK 2

(a)   C

(b)

	Basis of apportionment	Plastic moulding £	Plastic extrusion £	Maintenance £	Stores £	Canteen £	Totals £
Depreciation of plant and equipment	CA of plant and equipment	45,000	90,000	0	0	0	135,000
Power for production machinery	Production machinery power usage (KwH)	7,500	10,000	0	0	0	17,500
Rent and rates	Floor space	4,750	4,750	2,375	7,125	4,750	23,750
Light and heat	Floor space	1,250	1,250	625	1,875	1,250	6,250
Indirect labour	Allocated	0	0	10,000	12,500	36,000	58,500
Totals		**58,500**	**106,000**	**13,000**	**21,500**	**42,000**	**241,000**
Reapportion Maintenance		7,800	3,900	(13,000)		1,300	
Reapportion Stores		10,750	10,750		(21,500)		
Reapportion Canteen		21,650	21,650			(43,300)	
Total overheads to production centres		98,700	142,300				241,000

(c)

	Plastic moulding £	Plastic extrusion £
Budgeted overhead absorption rate	4.50 per hour	4.76 per hour

Plastic moulding = 22,500 ÷ 5,000 = £4.50 and Plastic extrusion = 24,750 ÷ 5,200 = £4.76.

(b)

	Actual hours worked	Absorbed amount £	Under/ over	Value £
Plastic moulding	5,000 × 1.05 = 5,250	£4.50 × 5,250 = £23,625	Over	£23,625 – £19,800 = £3,825
Plastic extrusion	5,200 × 1.03 = 5,356	£4.76 × 5,356 = £25,495	Under	£28,000 – £25,495 = £2,505

(c)

	Overhead absorption rate £	Overhead absorbed £	Under/over absorption £
Plastics moulding department	22,500 ÷ 15,000 = 1.50 per hour	1.50 × 14,500 = 21,750	21,750 – 19,800 = 1,950 over

TASK 3

(a)

Behaviour	Description
Variable cost	Increase in total as volume increases
Fixed cost	Decreases per unit as volume increases
Stepped cost	Fixed for a certain volume range only
Semi-variable cost	Made up of fixed and variable costs

(b)

Calculation of required number of litres	£	Marks
Fixed costs (W1)	55,000	3
Target profit	11,500	1
Fixed cost and target profit	66,500	2
Sales revenue	145,000	1
Variable costs (W2)	75,000	3
Contribution	70,000	2
Contribution per unit	14.00	2
Required number of litres to achieve target profit	4,750	2

Workings

(W1) Fixed costs = 20,000 + 15,000 + 20,000 = £55,000

(W2) Variable costs = 30,000 + 25,000 + (5,000 × £4) = £75,000

(c) $\frac{55,000}{14}$ = 3,928 litres

(d) 4,750 – 3,928 = 822 litres

TASK 4

(a)   **D**

(b)   **4 hours**

(c)

It helps coordinate the activities of different departments	✓
It establishes a system of control	✓
It fulfils legal reporting obligations	
It is a starting point for strategic planning	

(d)

	True	False
A flexible budget can be used to control operational efficiency	✓	
Rolling budgets review and, if necessary, revise the budget for the next period to ensure that budgets remain relevant for the remainder of the accounting period		✓

A flexible budget controls operational efficiency by producing a realistic budget cost allowance for the actual level of activity achieved. This allows a more meaningful control comparison with the actual results.

In a rolling budget system an extra period is added to the end of the budget when the most recent period has expired. The remaining budget might be updated at this point.

(e)

	Tick
Budgets can be used in situations where output cannot be measured, but standards cannot be used in such situations	✓
Budgets are used for planning purposes, standards are used only for control purposes	
Budgets can include allowances for inefficiencies in operations, but standards use performance targets which are attainable under the most favourable conditions	
Standards which remain unaltered for long periods of time are referred to as basic standards	✓

Standards can include allowances for inefficiencies in operations, through the use of attainable standards.

Standards and budgets are both used for planning and control purposes.

(f)

	days
Trade payables payment period	260,000/(1,650,000 × 90%) × 365 = 64
Inventory holding period	220,000/1,800,000 × 365 = 45

(g)

58 + 45 − 64 = 39 days

TASK 5

See MyKaplan for the full excel spreadsheet answers

	GG57 (£)	HH23 (£)	KK12 (£)	Total (£)
Selling price per unit	25.00	13.75	11.00	
Less: variable costs per unit:				
• Direct materials	7.50	5.25	3.00	
• Direct labour	8.75	4.00	2.00	
• Variable overheads	4.50	2.33	2.20	
Contribution per unit	4.25	2.17	3.80	
Sales volume (units)	1,000	1,500	1,875	
Total contribution	4,250	3,255	7,125	14,630
Less: fixed cost				12,750
Budgeted profit/loss				1,880
BEP	685	2,014	1,437	

TASK 6

See MyKaplan for the full excel spreadsheet answers

	Flexed budget	Actual	Variance
Volume sold	18,500	18,500	
Sales revenue	37,000	38,850	1,850
Less costs:			
Direct materials	14,800	17,575	−2,775
Direct labour	9,250	10,175	−925
Overheads	2,000	1,950	50
Operating profit	10,950	9,150	−1,800